MYTHS, LEGENDS, AND FOLKTALES FROM LATIN AMERICA

Golden Tales

RETOLD AND ILLUSTRATED BY
LULU DELACRE

SCHOLASTIC PRESS
NEW YORK

T O

Dianne Hess,
who helped me shape the clay

A N D T O

my husband, Arturo Betancourt,

A N D

my daughters, Verónica Elena and Alicia María,
for their relentless patience, understanding,
and encouragement

— L . D .

Heartfelt thanks for their help to Dr. Cecilia Capestany, Carolina Esteva, James Greensberg, John Hébert, Graciela Italiano, Marijka Kostiw, Tracy Mack, Teresa Mlawer, Priya Nair, Marta Orzábal Quintana, Dr. Ethel Ríos de Betancourt, Dr. Alberto Romo, Diana Sáez, Gaby Vallejo, and most specially to Dr. Georges Delacre, great educator and father.

The author wishes to thank Ione María Artigas de Sierra and Patrick McNamara for meticulously fact-checking the manuscript.

Library of Congress Cataloging-in-Publication Data

Delacre, Lulu.
Golden tales: myths, legends, and folktales from Latin America/Lulu Delacre.
p. cm.
Includes bibliographical references.
ISBN 0-590-48186-X
1. Legends — Latin America. 2. Indians — Folklore.
3. Indian mythology — Latin America. 4. Tales — Latin America. I. Title.
GR 114.D45 1996
398.2 '098 — dc20   94-36724
CIP

12 11 10 9 8 7 6 5 4 3 2 1   6 7 8 9/9 0/0 0/1
First printing, September 1996   46
The display type was hand lettered by Lulu Delacre.
The text type was set in Garamond No. 3.
The paintings in this book were done in oil over primed canvas.

Table of Contents

Latin America

United States
of America

TEXAS

Gulf of Mexico

FLORIDA

Bahamas

Mexico

Dominican
Republic

MEXICO
CITY

Cuba

SAN JUAN

Haiti

Belize

OAXACA

Puerto Rico

Jamaica

Hispaniola

Guatemala

Honduras

Caribbean Sea

Lesser Antilles

El Salvador

Nicaragua

Trinidad
and Tobago

Costa Rica

Venezuela

Guyana

French
Guiana

Panama

Suriname

BOGOTÁ

Pacific Ocean

Colombia

Atlantic Ocean

QUITO

Ecuador

Peru

Brazil

LIMA

CUZCO

Lake Titicaca

Current country boundaries are shown.

LA PAZ

Bolivia

RED AREA IN MAP BELOW
SHOWS LATIN AMERICA

GRAN CHACO

Paraguay

NORTH
AMERICA

NATIVE TRIBES
INCLUDED IN THE BOOK

Chile

SOUTH
AMERICA

TAINO

ZAPOTEC

MUISCA

Argentina

INCA

Uruguay

SANTIAGO

BUENOS AIRES

Introduction

The Americas were inhabited by scores of different native tribes when the Spaniards arrived in 1492. Each Indian tribe was a nation unto itself, with its own culture and language. Among them were the hospitable Taino Indians, who had established themselves in the islands of Puerto Rico, Hispaniola (which today contains the countries of the Dominican Republic and Haiti), Cuba, Jamaica, and the Bahamas. Also among them were the Zapotec Indians, who were master builders living in Mexico. There were the Muisca Indians from Colombia, who were renowned as goldsmiths, and there were the Inca, who had built a great empire spanning Ecuador, Peru, Bolivia, Chile, and Argentina.

First in search of wealth for the royal treasury, and later with the hope of converting the native people to Christianity, the Spaniards changed the face and character of the Americas in ways that are still felt today. Part of their legacy is the Spanish language, part is their Catholic religion, and part is their European culture, which has blended in many degrees with each different native culture.

Today, Latin America possesses a wealth of both pre-Columbian myths from the different native tribes, and legends and folktales that evolved after the Spanish arrival. In the following pages you will find twelve golden myths, legends, and folktales filled with the beauty and magic that reflect this fascinating and colorful history.

Give yourself up to a voyage of wonder. Starting in the Caribbean, then traveling southward to Bolivia, sample the lore that first originated with the Taino, the Zapotec, the Muisca, and the Inca. Then see how it changes as it blends with the Spanish culture, to become part of the Latin American literature we know today.

AGUACATE · AREPA · ATOL · BOHIO · BORIQUEN · CANOA · CAYO · CEIBA · CUBA · GUACAMAYO · GUARAGUAO · GUAYACAN · GUIRO · HABANA · HAITI · HAMACA · HUCAR · JUEY · MAJE · MANI · MARACA · YAGUA · YAGRUMO · YAREY · ZEMI

Mam...
Papayas
Quenepas
Guayabas
Yautia
Yuca
Boniato

From the Lands of the Taino

ABOUT THE TAINO

The Taino Indians were the native people of Puerto Rico, Hispaniola, Cuba, Jamaica, and the Bahamas. They were called "Taino" because several members of the tribe said that word to Columbus to indicate they were not aggressive like other tribes from the nearby islands. "Taino" means "good" or "noble" in Arahuaco, their native language.

The inhabitants of Puerto Rico and Hispaniola were the most advanced culturally among the Taino. They were accomplished farmers who lived in permanent villages, and were governed by a chief or *cacique*.

It has been chronicled that there were more than 600,000 Taino in the Caribbean around the time of Columbus's arrival. However, they no longer exist, having perished due to forced labor, wars, and European diseases to which they were not immune.

Today, the presence of the Taino people can still be felt. Some of their words, commonly used in the Spanish language, are still spoken in areas where the Taino lived. They are present in the carvings of wood, bone, and shell, in the stonework and pottery they left behind, and also in a number of food crops which they introduced to the Europeans. And as the Spaniards had freely intermixed with the Taino women, they left behind many mixed-race children. But perhaps the Taino spirit is felt the most in the welcoming nature of the Caribbean people.

How the Sea Was Born

A Taino Myth

In the mists of ancient times when the world was new and filled with the earliest Taino gods, there was Yaya. Yaya was the essence, the origin of life, the creator. Yaya was the great spirit.

He had a wife, and a son who was named Yayael. The three of them lived together in peace. Yayael was an obedient son who did everything he was told. But when the boy grew up, things changed. He had learned to think for himself and did not always agree with or even like what his father, the great spirit, told him. In fact, Yayael became such a strong-willed boy that he stopped following Yaya's commands altogether. He did what he pleased when he pleased. He talked back to his father, and showed such great disrespect that his father lashed out in anger.

"Leave home at once!" the wounded god told his son. "And do not return for four moons."

So it was done. Yayael left, and after four months he returned home. But this was not enough time to heal Yaya's deep torment, and he killed his turbulent-spirited son. With great anguish and sorrow, Yaya collected Yayael's bones and carefully placed them inside a hollow pumpkin gourd. Next, he hung the gourd high from the roof of his *bohío*, his hut. And that is where they remained.

3

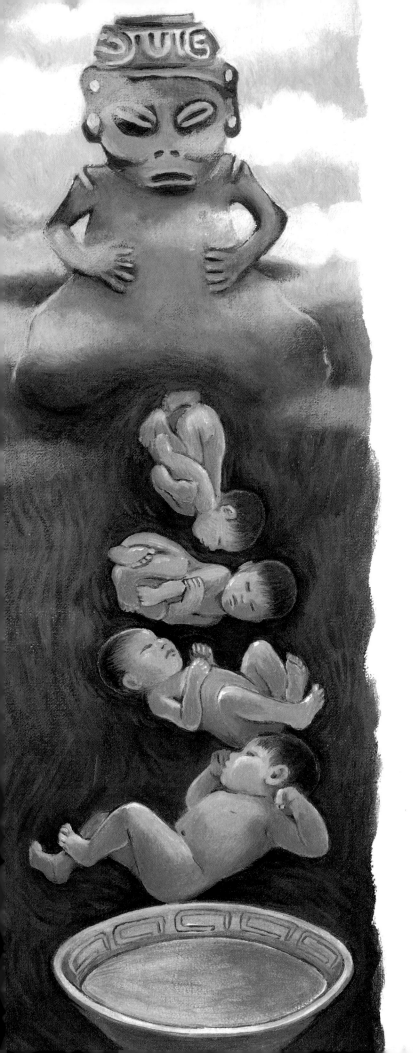

As time passed, Yaya longed to see his son again. So one day, with his wife by his side, he took down the gourd, and they peeked inside. To their amazement, the bones had disappeared! Instead, swimming inside the bowl were many fish of all shapes, sizes, and colors. There were big fish, small fish, thin fish, fat fish, silver fish, gold fish, and rainbow-colored fish, too. At first they didn't know what to make of this. They gave it a great deal of thought, and as the fish were fresh and plentiful, they decided to eat them. But for every fish they ate—another grew back in its place!

Nearby, in the stillness of the air, a piercing scream was heard. Then a second scream followed, then a third, then a fourth. Mother Earth, Itiba Cahubaba, had given birth to four identical babies, four divine children.

Itiba's firstborn was a rough-skinned baby, so she named him Deminán Cara-caracol. Deminán was very curious and fearless. As he was a natural leader, his brothers followed him everywhere.

Ever since he was a small boy, Deminán heard stories about Yaya, and he was determined to learn more about the powerful spirit. Once he saw Yaya leave his *bohío*. He followed him to his *conuco*, his vegetable garden. In this garden Yaya tended his corn and his yucca. Deminán noticed he did this every morning. So early one day, he and his brothers waited close by. As soon as Yaya had gone to care for his corn and yucca, Deminán Caracaracol swiftly led his brothers to the hut and snuck inside. There, hanging high from the roof, they discovered the magic gourd. When they took it down, they saw fish of all shapes, sizes, and colors still swimming inside. The fish looked so delicious, they could not resist eating them. And just as they were about to finish their delicious meal, Deminán felt the approaching presence of Yaya. Fearing punishment, the children quickly tried to hang the gourd back in its place. But the gourd slipped and crashed to the ground, breaking into many, many pieces.

Suddenly, a torrent of water gushed from the broken gourd. It spilled over the earth, and covered it with rivers, lakes, oceans, and seas. With the crashing waves and flowing streams came swimming and rushing fish of all shapes, sizes, and colors. There were big fish, small fish, thin fish, fat fish, silver fish, gold fish, and fish of all colors of the rainbow. There was water and fish in infinite quantities.

And this is how, from Yayael's bones, the sea was born.

It is said that the Taino Indians would hang a basket containing a man's skull from one of the bohío's *posts. This was done around the time the days grew a little shorter and the sun was not as hot. They did so to have a bountiful fishing season, and to remember their slain hero's bones from which the sea was born.*

Guanina

A Puerto Rican Legend, 1511

The evening golds and reds of the Caribbean sun glittered against Guanina's dark skin. But even the light's beautiful reflections that fell across her face could not hide the fear in her eyes. She had hidden the news for too long now, as she was torn between loyalty to her people and the deep love she felt for Don Cristóbal de Sotomayor, the Spanish *conquistador*.

Guanina was the niece of Agüeybana, the great Taino *cacique*, the great Taino chief. Three years earlier, he had welcomed the Spanish conquerors to the island of Boriquén. He had treated them with great hospitality, and had even let Don Cristóbal build a home in his own village. But now things were beginning to change.

When Guanina hastily entered her lover's grand house, she found him seated by the window. He seemed sad, as he often did now, staring off into the distance, lost in memories of his noble and courtly past in faraway Spain.

"What is wrong, my beautiful Guanina?" he asked, as he realized she was next to him. "Why is there fear in those eyes that are always so bright and full of life?"

"You must flee at once, my love," she whispered. "All the great chiefs of Boriquén are plotting to kill you! I know of caves that are hidden in the depths of our island. Please let me hide you in one of them!"

"My darling, foolish Guanina. Your people have been conquered. They will not rebel. They are weak, like a tree that has been bent and broken. They will never stand strong again."

Guanina's black eyes burned fiercely. "We believed the Spaniards were our friends. But we have been deceived. The Spaniards have degraded and enslaved my people. They have forced them to comb the mines for gold to enrich the Spanish treasury!"

"I see you are rebellious, my darling," he said, kissing her tenderly on the forehead, and pulling her close to him.

Guanina softened. "I am only saying what I feel, my lord. And I feel compelled to save you from this death sentence. Because I love you. And I don't want to see you die."

Just then, Juan González, the only Spaniard to fully understand Arahuaco, the Taino language, entered into the privacy of their world.

"My Captain!" he said. "The Taino are plotting a violent rebellion. I have just witnessed their *areito*, and during their ritual ceremony, they swore by your death in dance and song! We must flee immediately—and in secret— to the safety of Villa Caparra."

For a moment Guanina felt a flicker of hope, but it faded quickly.

"I will not flee or hide!" Don Cristóbal shouted. "I am a Sotomayor and will not be called a coward!"

She heard González try in vain to reason with Don Cristóbal. But, as she knew too well, it was of no use.

"Now leave me alone, González!" Don Cristóbal shouted. "Be gone with you!" He was determined to leave proudly the next morning, escorted by the people who threatened to kill him.

Sadly, Guanina's eyes drifted from Don Cristóbal's angry, reddened face to the window overlooking the sea. Numbly she rebraided her hair in the Castilian style as her lover had taught her. Once more she wished the Spaniards had never come. Once more she mourned for the peaceful quiet of times past that might never return.

When the interpreter was gone, Don Cristóbal beckoned Guanina to come to him. He clasped her hands close to his heart and, as the night's dark blanket shrouded the island, they fell into a long, bittersweet embrace.

The next day, in the stillness of the dawn, Juan González knocked softly on the door. "We have guarded you while you slept, my Captain," he said. "But time has run out. We must leave right away!"

"Bring the *cacique*, Guaybana," Don Cristóbal responded harshly.

González obeyed.

Guaybana was Guanina's brother. He had inherited the position of *cacique* from his uncle, the great chief, Agüeybana. But unlike his generous and hospitable uncle, Guaybana hated the white foreigners. And he had vowed revenge.

As Guaybana entered the room, he glared at his sister and greeted Don Cristóbal coldly.

"Guaybana," Don Cristóbal ordered the chief. "Get me a group of your *naborias*, a group of your servants, to escort me to Villa Caparra. I need them immediately!"

González translated his captain's orders, and as soon as the Taino chief had left, the interpreter revealed his anguish to Don Cristóbal.

"Why, my Captain, did you tell him our destination?" González shouted. "They will surely ambush us now!"

"Of course not, my good González," Don Cristóbal replied stiffly. "Now they will know we are not afraid of them. Besides, God will accompany us as he always has before."

The Taino servants arrived to carry Don Cristóbal's belongings. Guanina felt their cold stares. Their obvious anger and resentment for her tore at her heart and her spirit. They left the room and joined the small group of Christian travelers that was gathered outside in the courtyard waiting for further instructions.

As Don Cristóbal dressed himself in full armor, Guanina watched him with swollen eyes. She had begged him to take her along, but he refused, fearing for her safety. "I will return to you, my love," he whispered. "I promise you, I will return."

Silently they embraced once more, for a long moment of passion. Fully possessed by his love, she knew his heart was forever hers.

And as Don Cristóbal walked away, leaving her with a void in her heart, he wiped the tears from his own eyes. The arrogant soldier did not want his companions to see. But it was indeed a just tribute to the beautiful Guanina, who had sacrificed her loyalty to her home and her people for his love.

So it was that the Spanish captain and his small traveling group left in the coolness of the early tropical morning. As soon as they were gone, Guaybana gathered 300 of his best warriors and made an impassioned speech to them:

"Friends, our time has come. We can no longer stand the oppression. We must rebel against the invaders or die trying. Let's brandish our clubs and carry our bows and arrows. We will meet other warrior friends from the island. The great spirit of Cemí, the protector, is with us. Let us go!"

Guaybana led the way, following Don Cristóbal's trail. Wearing his feather headdress and his *guanín*, a large gold pendant on his chest, Guaybana was followed by a riotous group of warriors who screamed and shouted, ravenous for revenge.

Finally, they had lost their fear of the foreigners.

The first one to notice the approaching danger was González. As he stopped suddenly to listen to the loud noises coming from behind him, it was too late. Guaybana's men had viciously attacked him. With his head badly gashed and bleeding, González knelt before the Taino and begged for a pardon, promising to be forever in their service. They did not care for his offer. But nevertheless, they spared the life of the traitorous Spaniard.

Guaybana, the chief, gave orders to take a shortcut through the tropical forest to get to Don Cristóbal.

Very soon, Don Cristóbal and his five warriors also heard frightening sounds in the wind. It was then that Cristóbal realized that both Guanina and González had told the truth. But, as always, Cristóbal was proud of his noble lineage and fiercely loyal to his cause. He would not surrender. He would fight to the end!

"Men," he said to his fellow Christians. "We need to fight with all our might. We may be outnumbered, but together we shall win. May God be with us!"

"*Viva* Sotomayor!" his men cheered with fervor.

All of a sudden, from deep within the forest, scores of Taino warriors charged from all directions, engulfing the small Spanish contingent like a flood.

The battle was a bloody one. Both the Spanish and the Taino fought courageously to defend their own very different causes. The air was heavy with screams and shouts, and anguished cries. When the whirlwind of Taino clubs and Spanish swords ended, the ground was covered with corpses.

The last to fall was Don Cristóbal. Trying in vain to reach Guaybana, he was stopped suddenly by the heavy blows of a club. The first blow took his sword; the last took his life.

At battle's end, Guaybana gathered his men on a nearby hill to rest and bury their dead.

"We must admit the Spaniards fought with great valor to the end. Especially their Christian *cacique*, Don Cristóbal. As a great warrior he deserves a proper burial. Go get his body at once."

At the moment of Cristóbal's lethal blow, a sharp pain seized Guanina's heart. She ran through the forest to find him, but found only his lifeless corpse. Blinded by anguish, she knelt down beside him, and covered him

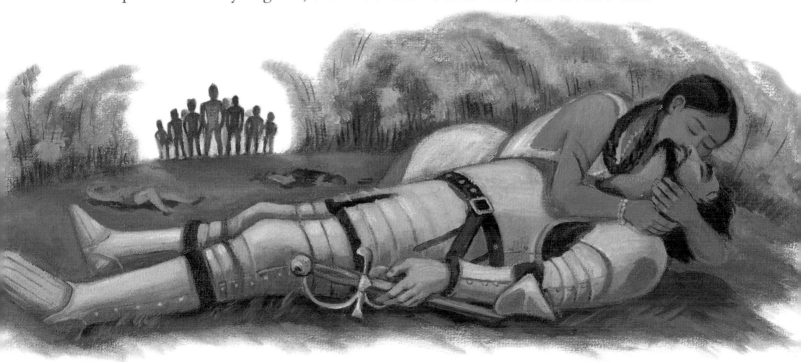

with kisses and tears, as if her devotion alone could restore his life.

This is how the twenty Taino Indians that her brother had sent found Guanina. She could not see clearly, her vision was blurred with tears, her whole body wracked by the shock of her lover's death. Screaming deliriously, she refused to let them take her beloved away.

When they returned to Guaybana and told him that his sister had prevented their taking the captain's body, Guaybana became somber and saddened.

"We must respect her pain," he said. "Since it is her will to remain with him, tomorrow at dawn she shall be sacrificed. She will then be laid on top of him, and they shall be buried together."

The next morning Guaybana set out for the site where the Spaniard was slain. There they found Guanina lying peacefully by his side. Upon trying to wake her, Guaybana realized the stillness of her body was beyond sleep. During the evening, Guanina had died.

The bodies of Guanina and Don Cristóbal de Sotomayor were buried at the foot of a huge old ceiba tree. It is said that in the very spot they were buried, fragrant white lilies and wild red poppies grow year after year, as if nature itself honors the love of two pure souls.

> Now, every evening around dusk,
> when the sky is painted in reds
> and the tree's shadows stretch far beyond their grave,
> local countrymen say you can hear voices
> carried by the wind.
> And when they hear the sweet love songs
> mixed with the rustling of leaves,
> they know then,
> with the setting sun as their only witness,
> that the spirits of the beautiful, determined Taino princess
> and her courageous Spanish warrior
> come out of their graves
> to share their intense love
> and kiss once more under the soft moonlight.

In 1508, the Spanish, under the leadership of Juan Ponce de León, started arriving on the island of Boriquén, which we now call Puerto Rico. They came to conquer the island in search of its gold and also to convert the Taino Indians who lived there to Christianity. There were around 60,000 Taino living in Puerto Rico when the Spaniards arrived. And by the time Spain accorded them freedom from slavery in 1542, only 60 remained.

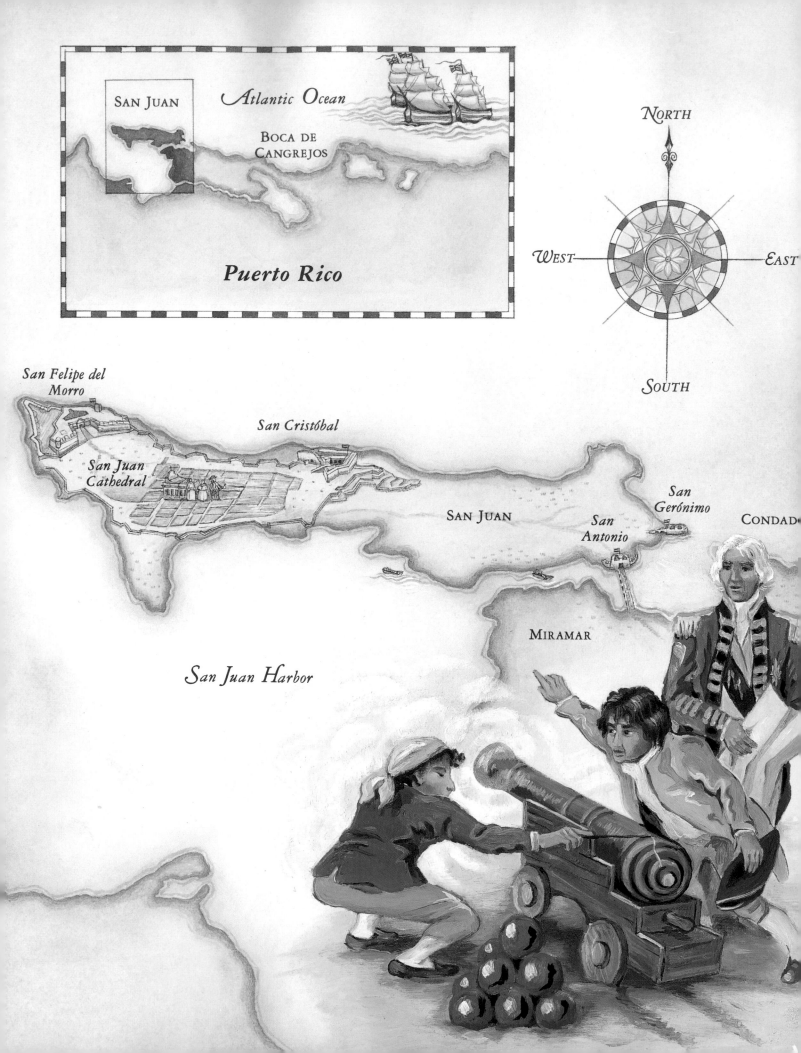

SAN JUAN

Atlantic Ocean

BOCA DE
CANGREJOS

Puerto Rico

NORTH

WEST — EAST

SOUTH

*San Felipe del
Morro*

San Cristóbal

*San Juan
Cathedral*

SAN JUAN

*San
Gerónimo*

*San
Antonio*

CONDAD

MIRAMAR

San Juan Harbor

The Eleven Thousand Virgins

A Puerto Rican Legend, 1797

In the year 1797, when pirates in swift-sailing tall ships ruled the seas, there lived an English general named Sir Ralph Abercromby. Abercromby had sailed to the Caribbean Sea with a fleet of over sixty ships and an army of fourteen thousand men. Upon his arrival, he quickly conquered the island of Trinidad. With new confidence and courage, he set out to win even more territory for England. This time he decided to take on the beautiful Spanish colony of Puerto Rico. That same year, his fleet set anchor in front of Boca de Cangrejos, near San Juan, the island's capital city.

Startled by the sudden appearance of warships and foreseeing a brutal attack, Don Ramón de Castro, Puerto Rico's governor at the time, immediately called his troops to arms. Preparations were made to defend the city. The bridge of San Antonio, which was the only access to the island city, was blocked. Groups of light boats loaded with artillery and cannons surrounded the walled city. Mounted patrols were sent nearby to the countryside to prevent pillaging and looting. And finally, women, children, and the elderly were ordered to flee inland for safety. Only able-bodied men were left to defend San Juan. The Catholic bishop, Trespalacios, who was in charge of the diocese, helped the governor with money and even loaned him men of

the cloth to help with the fighting at the trenches. Now the cross and the sword were united to fight the common enemy.

It was impossible to prevent the British soldiers from landing. Their anchored vessels sprayed the beaches with heavy shrapnel fire, allowing hundreds of small boats to bring mercenaries ashore. General Abercromby set up headquarters near the island city. Encouraged by his strong position, he continued west, determined to move forward until he reached the San Antonio bridge. Upon arrival, however, he was forced to stop. The cannon fire coming from the small San Antonio fort and from the San Gerónimo castle, a little to the north, was too heavy. The British army then set up trenches in both Miramar and Condado, the closest points to the city island. The battle that followed was fierce. The English cannons fired relentlessly, but the defense was persistent. For twelve consecutive days of constant fire, there was chaos and destruction, but nothing was gained for either party.

On the thirteenth day, the chancellor went to talk to the bishop.

"Your eminence," he said, "the men defending the city are very tired. They are far outnumbered by the English, and there is widespread fear that the city will succumb. Only a miracle could help us now. Let us organize a *rogativa*, a public prayer to beg for mercy from Heaven."

"Yes. A worthy idea," answered Bishop Trespalacios. "We will pray to Saint Catherine, who is the saint of the day, and to Saint Ursula and the eleven thousand Virgins. I'm especially devoted to them."

So it was decided right then that the entire city would participate in the magnificent event. Heralded by the sound of every church bell in the city, the rich, the poor, the peasants, the soldiers, and the priests alike, would all join in a long procession. Holding either candles or torches and led by the bishop, the clergy, and the city authorities, they would start at the cathedral and travel the city streets through the night. When dawn broke, they would return to where they began for a choral Mass, which would be accompanied by a full orchestra.

So at dusk on the evening of that thirteenth day of the siege, the procession took place. As the English sentries watched from their trenches, they realized there was unusual movement and activity inside the city. They could hear an eerie chorus of church bells ringing out loudly and incessantly. They also noticed many lights moving along to the west. One worried sentinel reported these findings to General Abercromby.

"They must be getting additional forces from inland," said Abercromby. "Our frigates at the entrance of the port can't get any closer because of the heavy cannon fire coming from the big fort guarding the San Juan Harbor. Let's increase the offensive in both Miramar and Condado," he ordered, "and sustain the musket fire against the gunboats!"

The general's orders were followed, and for a full three hours, the English offensive was mercilessly intensified. At midnight, the sentry returned to talk to the general.

"The lights inside the city are quickly multiplying, and now they seem to be coming toward us!"

The general called for an emergency meeting.

"We've been fighting for a long time now," he told his men, "but we haven't advanced an inch. The defense of the city hasn't weakened. And it seems as if forces have come from inland to its rescue. The drinking water here is very poor. Dysentery is ravaging our soldiers. I

think the time has come to return our troops to the ships."

The officers unanimously agreed, and the decision was final. By dawn on the first of May, the siege was over.

Meanwhile, at the cathedral, the choral Mass took place. Afterward, all voices were raised in unison with the hymn "Te Deum," and Bishop Trespalacios gave a long sermon.

Those who were there swore to the triumph of Saint Ursula and the eleven thousand Virgins. They said that on that sleepless night of prayer and hope, the English cannons fired more shells than ever before, shells that never reached the city, because they mysteriously reversed their direction. They also said that when the long procession of clergymen, soldiers, and peasants holding their lighted candles and torches finally reached the cathedral, all cannon fire suddenly stopped, and the Englishmen vanished.

Some say that the tenacity and experience of the small Spanish garrison saved the city. Some say it was the courage and loyalty of the never-ending stream of armed peasants coming to the rescue from inland. Yet others strongly believe in the intervention of Saint Ursula and the eleven thousand Virgins.

Today, near the Old San Juan Gate close to the cathedral, stands a bronze sculpture called La Rogativa. It commemorates the miraculous vigil of that night when only courage, faith—and eleven thousand lights—saved the city.

Oh tú que pasando vas
Fija los ojos en mí
Cual tú te ves yo me vi
Cual yo me veo te verás

The Laughing Skull

A DOMINICAN LEGEND, 1836

Long ago, next to the Convent of Santo Domingo, stood a stone wall. Nestled in that wall was an empty niche. But the niche had not always been empty. It is said that since the seventeenth century when the church was built, a human skull was displayed there. Perched on an iron stand, it was quite visible during the day. By nightfall, it was well-illuminated by the oil lamp above it. And hanging just beneath this niche was an ordinary wooden sign that read:

> *Oh, you passerby—*
> *look at me, please.*
> *Like you I once was,*
> *Like me, you will be!*

As the years passed, people became so used to this sight that they walked right by the wall, ignoring the skull and the unusual inscription. That is, until one day, or rather one night, when a neighbor who lived near Hostos Street was on his way home. He heard some very strange noises coming from the skull, and he looked up. As his heart beat fast in sheer horror, he watched the skull nod once, then again, then shake its head as if it were at first

approving—then disapproving of his thoughts. He raced home in shock, gasping and whimpering all the way.

The news of this strange event spread like wildfire. And those who feared the sight of the skull, or those who had something to hide, wisely did not go near the convent. However, the daring and curious would wander by the church at night to see the frightening scene for themselves. Then they would later boast of their courage in great detail, telling of how the skull appeared to read their minds.

Once, some young boys who stayed late to watch the skull were quite sure they heard it laugh at them in a loud, shrill tone. Soon after, fear grew and grew in the neighborhood, as did the stories and gossip. People went far out of their way to avoid passing the wall. Since most odd things happened after dark, the lamplighter was careful to light the lamp while the sun was out. Eventually, even the military police would not dare go near the wall.

One very dark night, however, two soldiers patrolling the area decided to defy their own fear, and cautiously approached the convent. As they looked inside the niche, they saw it with their own eyes. The skull was shaking, back and forth, clattering loudly against the stone wall. Without thinking twice, the men fled in panic, and did not stop until they reached their headquarters. There they pounded desperately on the gate. And it was this that triggered the events that later would break the spell of the skull.

At this particular time, it happened that Abad Alfau was second lieutenant of the battalion that patrolled the main square of Santo Domingo. He was nineteen years old, and was a very handsome and bright lad, whom everybody called simply Abad. He was on duty the night the two soldiers fled from the horrifiying sight. Abad was very upset at the cowardice of the soldiers and sternly reprimanded them. The next evening, when he found out that yet another patrol had detoured from the frightening corner to avoid the laughing skull, he flew into a rage. "This will stop immediately," he said to himself, "or these cowards will be dismissed from the force!"

The following night, Abad ordered two soldiers to bring him a ladder. Two hours before midnight he removed his uniform and dressed in dark pants and a long, dark cape. Then he bravely marched to the wall on Hostos Street, brandishing his sword in his right hand. The two soldiers carrying the ladder followed sheepishly behind him.

They must have been about twenty feet from the niche in the wall when the skull began to shake, and laugh, and clatter, and moan. The noise was too much for one of Abad's companions, and he turned to flee.

"Stop!" cried Abad.

The soldier stopped as he was commanded.

"Now place the ladder in front of the niche," Abad ordered. The soldier did so.

Abad clung tightly to his sword and began to climb up. As he climbed higher, the noises became louder and louder. The skull shook once, twice, three times—until it began to spin violently. Chilling screeches emerged, screeches that would freeze the hearts of even the bravest of men. Oddly enough, Abad remained calm. He was determined to discover the mystery of the skull. As the soldiers held on firmly to the ladder, Abad reached the top. Slowly he lifted his weapon and, with the flat of his sword, he struck two heavy blows that sent the skull spinning and whirling and crashing to the ground.

It was this that unveiled the mystery. From beneath the skull, a horde of frightened mice scurried down the wall, onto the street, then into the darkness of the breezy island night.

People say that at dawn the broken skull was swept up by a street cleaner, and no one ever mentioned it again. Nearly seventy years later the ancient wall was demolished—and along with it, the empty niche.

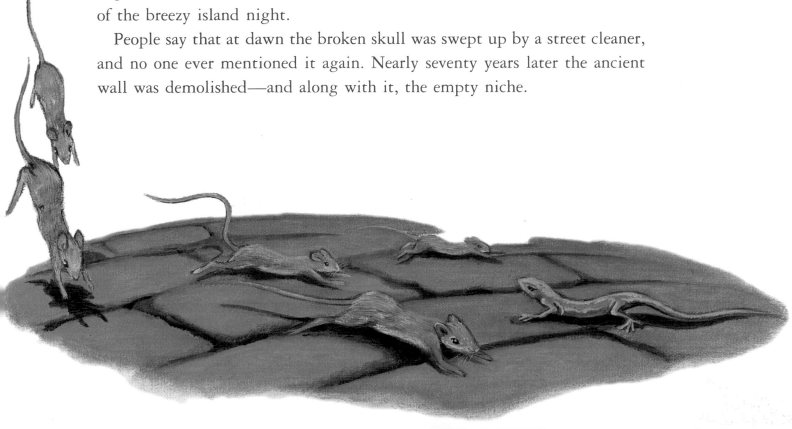

Sención, the Indian Girl

A Cuban Folktale, 1816

There once was a black man who lived with his old wife and their beautiful daughter. They lived together in a hut made of stalks and palm tree leaves, which they'd recently built on a picturesque site near the lagoon in Sagua la Grande.

Ascensión was the young girl's name, but her parents had lovingly nicknamed her Sención. Her skin, like her father's, was the color of rich, aromatic coffee, but her facial features displayed a mixture of the three races: white, black, and Indian. In fact, she was often called "The Indian Girl" because of her long, black, silky hair that was tightly woven into two long braids that fell gracefully over her shoulders. Although her exquisite beauty had made more than one young man fall in love with her, she had developed a strong and arrogant disposition.

There was one suitor in particular that Sención's parents strongly disliked. And it seemed that the more they disliked him, the more the couple wanted to be together.

It was to keep Sención far away from this persistent young man that her parents had moved to their current home in Sagua la Grande.

But it wasn't long before the boy discovered where his true love was hidden, and he rushed to see her. For many days, they secretly met by the grove next

to the lagoon, spending long hours exchanging words of passion and looks filled with desire.

One afternoon Sención's mother went to the lagoon for some water. As she was about to leave, she overheard some familiar voices by the grove. She looked around, and to her astonishment, she discovered the two lovers!

"How can you disobey your mother like this?" the old woman asked in a voice that trembled with sadness and indignation. When the boy heard her harsh words, he left quickly, burning with shame. But Sención did not do the same. As her mother spoke, she felt her blood boil, and her heart stirred with fury and anger.

"Mamaíta, you have humiliated me in front of my boyfriend!" she screamed. "You will not do it again!" And without even thinking, she opened her right hand and slapped her mother across the face.

"Wretched child!" the old woman whispered, her eyes welling up with tears. "God shall punish you."

And as these words were spoken, a most peculiar and mysterious thing happened. Sención's hand stuck to the old woman's face.

For several days Sención remained in deep distress until her worried father went to seek the help of a renowned medicine man, the one who was called only for the most urgent cases. When he arrived, he tried everything from potions to prayers, but still, nothing worked.

"There is no other way," the medicine man said at last. "The hand must be cut off."

During the painful operation, Sención did not scream or cry or even complain. She remained cold and unmoved. When the medicine man finished wrapping her wound in gauze, she got up, and without a word walked slowly to the edge of the lagoon. But she didn't stop. She kept right on walking until the waters covered her legs, her torso, her neck, then her face. Thus she disappeared into the lagoon forever.

Soon after, her father died. But the mother lived on for many years. She kept herself busy weaving fine hats made of palm leaves. And the old woman always made sure to hide the left side of her face from view, where Sención's hand, hardened by time, still remained attached—until her death.

Legend says that every first Friday of the full moon at exactly midnight, Sención rises from the lagoon more beautiful than ever before. Her silky, soft braids are still draped over her shoulders. Her arms are raised toward the sky as if begging forgiveness from God. And at the end of her right arm is the stump of her hand, still wrapped in the medicine man's gauze.

It is said that this peculiar event took place after Sagua la Grande was founded in the northern part of Cuba in 1814.

From the Land of the Zapotec

ABOUT THE ZAPOTEC

The Zapotec are one of the largest Indian groups in Mexico today. The different tribes, including the Chatino, live in many areas of the state of Oaxaca. Since there are sixteen Zapotec dialects, the tribes communicate with one another in Spanish. They are accomplished farmers and folk artists. And even though most are now Catholic, they still conduct their ancient rituals in hills and caves. There, they bring offerings to the god of lightning in hopes he will bring rain for an abundant harvest.

The Zapotec have inherited an illustrious past. They built the ancient city of Monte Albán that became the center of the classic civilization. Ruins dating from 500 B.C. still stand near the colonial city of Oaxaca. Pre-classic inscriptions found there suggest that remote ancestors of the Zapotec were the inventors of the pictographic writing later adopted by the Maya, the Mixtecs, and the Aztecs. They also built Mitla, the beautiful city that is considered one of the architectural wonders of ancient Mexico.

It should be mentioned as well that the legendary president Benito Juárez, the only full-blooded Indian to have governed Mexico since the pre-conquest times, was a Zapotec.

When the Sun and the Moon Were Children

A Chatino Myth

In ancient times, the sun and the moon were twin brother and sister, living as real children on earth. One day, as the children were out walking, they came upon the Night Terror. He was terribly jealous of the twins, and he wanted to do away with them. So he began to follow them everywhere they went.

Filled with fear, Sol, the little sun child, and Luna, the little moon child, ran and ran until they found a place to hide at the bottom of the river. Now this river was a part of the sea. And when the tide was low, and the river began to dry up, the children panicked.

Fortunately, just then, a little old lady came to fetch water from the river. The twins called out to her and told her all about the Night Terror, and the kind old lady offered to hide them. She placed each of them inside of one of her cheeks and headed home. On her way, she encountered the Night Terror.

"Why do you have such a round face?" he asked.

"I have a terrible toothache," said she.

And when he disappeared, the three of them laughed, as she had fooled the children's enemy.

The twins stayed at the old lady's home. She fed them, and took good care

of them, and brought them up as though they were her own. Most of the day she worked spinning cotton, and the rest of the day she spent alone in the dark woods. Whenever the old lady went outdoors, Sol and Luna were quite naughty. They would unravel and tangle what she had just spun, delighting in the look of shock on her face when she returned. Nevertheless, the three of them were happy together. Before long, the children came to believe that the little old lady was their mother.

As Sol and Luna grew up, they took a great interest in hunting. They made their own bows and arrows, and hunted all sorts of animals. They especially liked bringing pigeons home, for their mother prepared a delicious meal with them. Every now and then, the old lady would go into the woods, and Sol and Luna would always ask her where she was going.

"I am going to visit your father," she would respond.

As time passed, the children grew more and more curious about him, until finally one day they asked, "Mamá, who is our father?"

"He lives deep in the woods," she said. "But I must never tell you where, for fear you may hunt him."

Sol and Luna were puzzled, so the next morning when the old lady left to see her husband, the twins decided to follow her. They walked into the woods, carefully leaving behind a trail of small leaves and ashes to mark the way. As the old lady reached a clearing in the woods they heard her call out to her husband in a strange manner. Instantly a great deer appeared and she fed it with greens she had brought from home. Sol and Luna were very surprised when they realized the lady's husband was a deer. But they didn't want to get caught, so they ran back home and got there before her.

The next morning, the little old lady asked Sol and Luna to fetch some fresh grass clippings, telling them her husband only ate greens. The twins went to the field and made a big wooden blade to cut the grass. Sol swung the blade with such force that he scared a baby rabbit that was quietly hiding in the tall grass. The frightened rabbit leaped high out of the grass, hitting Luna, and forever imprinted its shape on her cheek. This is why you can see a rabbit's picture in the full moon.

The following day the twins decided to spy on the lady's husband, who was supposed to be their father. They snuck out of the house and carefully followed the trail of ashes and leaves they had left on the ground two days before. Once they got to the clearing in the woods, they mimicked the strange call they had heard Mamá make before. The great deer appeared.

"I don't believe he is really our father," whispered Sol to Luna.

"Look at its skinny legs," said Luna. "It is too ugly to be our father."

"We must kill it," they decided.

When the deer was close enough, Sol shot an arrow right through its heart. Then Sol and Luna cleaned the flesh from the carcass and grilled the innards to prepare a tasty dish known as *skualyku*. They ate everything but the liver. This was a delicacy they saved for Mamá.

Before leaving, Sol and Luna took the empty deerskin and filled it with hundreds of wasps; then they arranged it on the ground so it would look like a sleeping deer.

Upon returning home, they gave the liver to Mamá. She was delighted to have such a delicious thing to eat. Just as she was about to taste it, a scream came from the liver and then a toad croaked three times singing, "You are eating your husband's flesh." All this made Mamá very suspicious.

"Is it true what the toad just said?" the little old lady asked Sol and Luna. "Did you kill my husband?"

"No, Mamá," they replied. "Don't pay any attention to this gossip." But the old lady still felt uneasy, so she decided to go visit her husband.

Once she had gathered the freshest greens, she started on her way. First, she encountered a crab.

"The great deer is dead!" it told her.

This pained the old lady so much that she crushed the crab with her foot, which is why the crab is flat today. Then she continued on her journey.

Next, she encountered a pigeon. The pigeon sang *"Suliuu, suliuu,"* which in Chatino means: "It is lying down, it is lying down."

The old lady thanked the pigeon and went on her way.

Finally, she saw the deer lying down, just as the pigeon had said. Thinking that her husband was resting instead of working, she furiously scolded him and beat him with her staff. The sharp blows tore the deer's skin, and out of the hole came hundreds of angry wasps. They stung her over and over again, covering her with scores of painful bites. Screaming desperately, she ran away.

"Jump in the water, Mamá!" she heard the baby rabbit scream.

"No, I'd better go home to my children," she said. "They will make me a sweatbath."

When Mamá arrived, Sol and Luna quickly fixed her a sweatbath. They made a great big fire with lots of logs and layers of medicinal green leaves so the smoke would heal her. The fire roared, and the sweatbath became so hot that the little old lady perspired greatly, and soon she began to burn. She begged her children to take her out, but they refused.

"You must stay here, holy Mamá," Sol and Luna said. "From now on, you shall be the protector of all newborn children. New parents will bring food to sustain you, for this is your destiny." So the old lady stayed in the sweatbath and burned to ashes, and the twins then left for the hills.

Deep sadness overcame Sol and Luna. The more they thought about it, the more they realized how Mamá had lived and died in darkness. They wished there was some way to shed light upon her. They decided to climb the highest mountain up to the sky, and shine on her. Sol took his mother's staff while Luna took her skein of cotton thread. Suddenly, on their way up, they spotted an unusual serpent. It had big, luminous eyes. The children looked at each other and knew exactly what to do. Sol hit the serpent with the staff and Luna strangled it with the thread. Then they each took one of the bright, shining eyes. Luna kept the right one, which was also the brightest, and they continued their climb up.

A while later, Luna
saw a beehive. With the
help of the cotton thread
she lowered it from the
tree and drank the sweet
honey. It was so sweet it
made her very thirsty. Sol
drove his staff into the
ground, and water sprung from
the hole. Sol drank until he could
drink no more. Luna begged him for
a drink. Sol smiled mischievously and
told her that he would give her water if
she would trade her brighter serpent's eye for
his duller one. Luna was angered by his trick, but
being terribly thirsty, gave in. That is how the sun got to be brighter than
the moon.

When they reached the mountaintop, Sol took the cotton skein and threw
one end of it high into the sky. Holding on to the other end, Sol led the
way, because his light was brighter. Unhappily, Luna followed behind.

This is the way that the sun and the moon rose up into the sky. Today
they still constantly circle the heavens, always illuminating with both radiant
brilliance—and with soft moonlight—their mother's ancient grave.

*To this day, Chatino parents bathe their newborn babies in a sweatbath in memory
of the little old lady who is protector of all children. They make an offering of candles,
tortillas, tamales, and chickens during the ceremony. By doing this, they believe she
will protect their babies from illnesses the same way she protected Sol and Luna from
the Night Terror.*

How the Rainbow Was Born

A ZAPOTEC MYTH

Long ago, before there was light, there was Cosijogui, the god of lightning. He sat on his beautiful throne with four enormous clay pots at his feet. Each pot was guarded by a young lightning god who was disguised as a lizard.

The first pot hid all the world's clouds, the second hid all the world's water, the third hid all the world's hail, and the last one hid all the world's wind. The young lizard-guardians made sure to keep the contents of these mysterious pots secret.

"Cloud Guardian!" Cosijogui commanded one day. "Awaken the clouds! Let them come out from the pot!"

Although Cloud Guardian was surprised at Cosijogui's command, he promptly removed the lid, and soon the clouds spread across the dark sky. Cloud Guardian had never seen such a wondrous sight and he began playfully dancing with them. And each time he moved, lightning forked against the immense darkness.

At this time, the earth was still dark, and the men who inhabited it marveled at the sight of this grand spectacle. They were also very thirsty, so they prayed to the god of lightning to send them water instead of clouds.

"Water Guardian," Cosijogui commanded. "Open your clay pot and let the water come out!"

Water Guardian was also surprised at Cosijogui's command. But he did as he was told, and torrents of rain flooded the earth.

Meanwhile, Cloud Guardian continued dancing and tumbling through the sky, sending lightning streaks in all directions.

Now the women who inhabited the dark earth became frightened. They, too, prayed to the god of lightning, begging him to put an end to this terror. Cosijogui ignored them, so they sent some messengers to him. When these women arrived, they saw the other two sealed pots and grew very curious— so curious, that they forgot why they had come. Instead they asked the old god of lightning to open the pots and show them their secret contents. He smiled maliciously and initially refused, but the women continued to sweetly beg and plead so he finally gave in.

"Hail Guardian," the god of lightning commanded. "Open your pot at once!"

Out of the third pot came an avalanche of hard water stones, which pelted the earth with a vengeance. And as the hailstones fell, the other two lizard-guardians joined the Cloud Guardian in his frenzied dance. Together they celebrated their newly discovered freedom. This caused a disastrous tempest of thunder, lightning, rain, and hail, which grew worse with every movement.

Men, women, birds, and beasts alike were sure that the end of the world was near. So they prayed and pleaded with the god of lightning to calm the violent tempest. But Cosijogui and his lizard-guardians were enjoying their frenzied fun, ignoring the anguish of the earth's inhabitants. Then, in a final effort for peace, men, women, birds, and beasts raised their voices to Pitao, the great lord of the air. Pitao, with pity in his heart, commanded the dark clouds of the east to give way to the strongest god of all—Gabicha, the sun.

The fiery golden star appeared in the horizon. Its strong light broke through the clouds. Panic overcame the god of lightning, so awed was he by the sight of the new star. He had long been the supreme god of the sky, and he knew now that Gabicha's blinding strength would overtake his own power over the heavens.

Silently and disconsolately Cosijogui watched as Gabicha asked the last lizard-guardian to open up the remaining clay pot. This one would release the wind that would blow the tempest away. Wind Guardian obeyed. He opened the pot and, in a single breath, the wind tore the clouds away. Then, following Gabicha's command, Wind Guardian called his brothers who had unleashed the tempest and told them to humbly return to their posts.

In the stillness of the moment, the old lightning god saw how truly great the sun was, and he knew he would never again rule over the skies. As time passed, the sun earned Cosijogui's deepest respect. For now he could see the sun was a kind, just, and generous god—a god who loved all the men, women, birds, and beasts that inhabited the new bright world.

So Cosijogui thought of a way to pay homage to the mighty new god. He would lay a multicolored bridge over the immense space between the sky and the earth. It would be a gift to Gabicha to help him climb down and bring all the men, women, birds, and beasts on earth his message of peace.

And this is how the rainbow was born.

The Miracle of Our Lady of Guadalupe

A MEXICAN LEGEND, 1531

On the ninth of December in 1531, just ten years after the Spanish conquest, a miracle occurred. It all began when Juan Diego, a poor and devout young Aztec Indian, was on his way to catechesis. While walking through the bushes in the hills of Tepeyac, he passed the ruins of a temple that was dedicated to Tonantzin of Tepeyac. She was the Aztec mother of gods and patroness of midwives and healers. It was said that in the old times, Aztec pilgrims traveled long distances to the temple in search of cures.

Juan Diego was thinking of this when suddenly a holy vision appeared. The most beautiful woman he had ever seen, with skin the color of the rich Mexican earth and a gaze that was filled with love and kindness, stood before him. Juan Diego was so awed by this that he slowly knelt down at her feet.

In her softest voice, the Virgin spoke to Juan Diego, for he had been chosen to deliver a request to Bishop Zumárraga. The Virgin wanted the bishop to build her a shrine on the very spot where she was standing. Juan Diego promised to deliver this message. But the moment he lifted his face from her feet, the Virgin had vanished.

Immediately he ran to see the bishop, but the bishop did not believe the boy's story, and he sent him on his way.

A few days later, while on the hills of Tepeyac, Juan Diego received a

second visit from the Virgin. And a second time she asked that the bishop build a church on the spot where she was standing. Again he delivered the Virgin's message, and again, the bishop dismissed him. But this time, the bishop told Juan Diego to bring a sign from the Blessed Lady if she were to come again.

On December twelfth, the Virgin appeared before Juan Diego a third time. He quickly told her that the bishop had requested a sign from her. She told him to gather some roses. And even though roses do not bloom in the hills of Tepeyac in December, Juan Diego found hundreds of them in full blossom, covering the hills nearby just as the Lady had promised. He picked them and placed the fragrant red flowers in the fold of his coarsely woven cloak.

That very day, he went for his third meeting with the bishop. The bishop welcomed him, and as Juan Diego opened his cloak to drop the fresh roses at the bishop's feet, something extraordinary happened. There, imprinted on the front of his cloak in all her beauty, was the image of Our Blessed Virgin of Guadalupe. Astonished, Bishop Zumárraga gave orders for a shrine to be built in the hills of Tepeyac as the Lady had requested. And in 1709 the old Basilica of Guadalupe was completed—right where the temple to the Aztec mother of gods had stood.

Spaniards and Indians alike have passionately worshipped the Mexican Virgin for centuries. In what is now called "La Villa de Guadalupe," the old basilica stands with the new basilica by its side.

The number of pilgrims who visit the site grows yearly. Maybe it is because the Lady grants so many cures and favors, or maybe it is because she blesses the blending of cultures and races by her mere existence. Or perhaps it is because her wonderful story is retold again and again outside the entrance to the new basilica to all those who wish to listen.

Inside the new basilica, Juan Diego's cloak hangs in a golden frame at the altar. After more than 400 years, the image is still intact. If you ever go there, look closely at the Virgin's eyes. For there you may very well see the face of the Indian, Juan Diego, reflected deep within them.

Since 1910, Our Lady of Guadalupe has been the Patroness Saint of Hispanic America.

From the Land of the Muisca

ABOUT THE MUISCA

At the time of the Spanish conquest, the Muisca Indians, sometimes also called Chibcha, occupied the Andean plateau in Colombia. They farmed the land and were skilled goldsmiths and pottery makers.

Sun and water worshippers, the population gathered from time to time at ceremonial centers where gold played an important role. Exquisite gold figurines shaped to represent humans and animals were deposited as offerings in temples and sacred lagoons.

The Muisca were easily conquered by the Spaniards, and by the eighteenth century their native language, Chibcha, had virtually disappeared. Many intermarried with the Spanish. And although they did not leave any architectural monuments, the gold relics, the ancient pottery, and the magic rituals that are still practiced in the *barrios* of Bogotá today remind us of their rich heritage.

El Dorado

A COLOMBIAN LEGEND, SIXTEENTH CENTURY

Sebastián de Benalcázar, founder of Quito in Ecuador, was a very ambitious conquistador. *He had a network of Indian informants that periodically brought him news of rich lands still to be conquered. Around the year 1534, an informant told him of a hidden place said to be filled with golden treasures. Benalcázar named the place* El Dorado, *meaning the "golden one," after hearing the Indian tell this story:*

Deep at the bottom of the Guatavita Lagoon lives a glittering serpent. Some say the serpent is the goddess Bachué, mother of the Muisca. Others swear it is the devil himself. But what *is* true is that for a long time, the Muisca Indians had been showering the lagoon's serpent with gold and emeralds to show their reverence and adoration and to curry favors from it. This was the custom during the reign of the great Muisca chief of Guatavita.

The Guatavita chief was married to a maiden of unsurpassed beauty. He had loved her dearly, at least for a while. But in time, the splendor of his kingdom and the many other beautiful women that surrounded him began to compete for his attention. And before long he started to neglect her.

The chief's wife resented being ignored in such a way. When a high-ranking Indian from her husband's court fell in love with her, she returned his passion. Soon their love became so compelling that they forgot all about

her husband, the most powerful of the Muisca—and about the fact that she was the mother of their only daughter.

One day, her husband found out about her unfaithfulness. Blinded by rage and obsessed with revenge, he ordered the cruelest punishments he could think of. First he had her lover killed. Then he spread word about what she had done. Worst of all, at the chief's lavish, royal parties, his subjects sang of her shameless conduct. They repeated the disgraceful stories so many times that humiliation overwhelmed her.

One moonless night she fled the village to escape her torturous punishment. Holding her baby daughter tightly in her arms, she ran toward the only source of consolation she knew—the Guatavita Lagoon. She looked for a long while into the black and still waters, and instead of making an offering of gold or jewels, as was the custom, she threw her baby in. Then she jumped in herself. They both drowned.

The *jeques*, the guardian priests of the lagoon, were sleeping in their huts on the bank when they heard the loud commotion. They came out right away, but it was too late. Mother and child had already disappeared deep into the bottom of the waters. At dawn in the early morning light, they confirmed their worst fears. The wife of the chief of Guatavita and her baby daughter were dead. Quickly one of the *jeques* ran to inform her husband of the tragic event.

The chief was shocked by the news, and immediately rushed to the lagoon. He stood there for a moment dumbstruck, watching in disbelief. After a while, he ordered the highest priest to go into the lagoon and retrieve his wife and daughter.

The *jeque* tried his most powerful ceremonies and rites. He lit a fire near the water's edge and placed some cobblestones in it. Once the stones were as hot as the fire itself, he threw them into the lagoon. Then, removing his clothes, he jumped in and dove after the stones. The chief was waiting outside when the high priest finally came out from the water.

"Your wife is alive and well," he said. "She lives next to the serpent of the lagoon in a better place than before. She told me she and her daughter are happy where they are and do not wish to return."

"This cannot be!" exclaimed the chief. "Go back to the depths of the lagoon and don't return without my daughter!"

So the high priest went in once more and then returned to the surface, this time with the tiny lifeless body of the chief's baby. She was missing her eyes, for the serpent had taken them to render the baby useless to the humans. This way the serpent made sure she would return to her mother's side to be raised properly in the underwater world.

"Let the serpent's wish be a command," said the chief sadly. "Return my daughter to the lagoon." Then, overwhelmed by sadness, guilt, and longing, the chief watched his daughter as she sank into the waters once again. And, as she sank, he realized, perhaps too late, the greatness of the love he had always felt for his wife and child.

It was at this painful moment that the chief of Guatavita promised his wife he would offer the serpent of the lagoon more than he ever had before. This way he would win its favor and make sure his wife's afterlife would be as happy as their first years had been together. Quickly the word spread among the Muisca that the chief was planning the most lavish ceremony yet. This time it was for his wife who lived by the serpent's side at the bottom of the lagoon.

The chief began a fasting period along with his attendants. This would purify their bodies and souls so they would be worthy of worshipping the goddess of the lagoon.

Meanwhile, preparations for the grand occasion were under way. The whole village would participate in the festivities. The most delicate foods and the most exquisite *chicha* drink were prepared with golden corn. The robes and headdresses were carefully assembled. Masks were cleaned and musical instruments tuned. The excitement mounted as the time for the religious ceremony and the great feast after it neared.

At dawn of the day, the chief was ready. His robe was removed and his servants spread a sticky substance all over his skin. Then they covered his body with powdered gold. Once the solemn moment had passed, he wore his royal robe and slowly walked to the beautiful raft that was waiting at the bank of the lagoon.

People had come from all over to witness the sacred and flamboyant cere-mony. His warriors and other subjects scattered richly colored pieces of cloth at his feet so the chief could walk upon them. He got to the bank and slowly stepped onto the oval raft. Some of his attendants accompanied him. He stood in the middle of the raft and removed his robe. He looked like a golden statue amidst the gold, jewelry, emeralds, culinary delicacies, and the many other treasures that surrounded him. These would be offered to the serpent of the lagoon in remembrance of his wife.

The raft moved away from the shore toward the center of the lagoon, then stopped. The chief invoked the gods, and after his prayer he threw the rich offerings, one by one, into the calm waters. After all the treasures had plunged into the lagoon, the chief jumped in, too. As a final offering to the aquatic temple, he rubbed the thick layer of gold off his body.

Finally he returned to the raft and was brought to shore. The chief walked to his attendants, who carried him to his hut. There the people, purified by the ceremony at the lagoon, felt free to fully enjoy the festivities that were about to begin.

This ritual became a tradition and was repeated many times at Guatavita Lagoon. Initially it was to ask favors from the serpent-goddess. Later it was a way to endow each new chief with great power.

Nobody knows whether the chief's wife was ever appeased by these magnificent rituals. But she well could have been. For the bottom of the lagoon was covered by a thick layer of gold, jewels, and emeralds—as proof of the chief's overdue but fervent love.

Upon hearing of these riches, the Spaniard Benalcázar decided to make the discovery his. In order to keep the location secret, he began to refer to the site as "El Dorado." But talk of this treasure spread far and wide, and by the time he arrived at Guatavita Lagoon, he found the area had already been conquered. Nevertheless, the story became widely known in Europe, and many adventurers who dreamed of instant riches traveled to the Americas in search of El Dorado.

From the Lands of the Quechua, Children of the Inca

ABOUT THE INCA

In 1532, the Spaniards arrived in Peru during the reign of Atahualpa, the last of the Inca rulers. They conquered the Inca empire and imposed their religion, their language, and their customs on its people. The widespread intermarriage between the Inca and the Spaniards created a new race called the Cholos.

Today, the Inca's presence is still strongly felt in the ruins of their ancient architectural sites like the Temple of the Sun in Cuzco and the citadel of Machu Picchu. It is also felt through the dominant language, Quechua, which was the language of the Inca. And the mythology that was passed along through the centuries still permeates the daily life of the present day highland peasants.

Even now, centuries after the arrival of Christianity, the Quechua Indians still identify God with the sun, and have made Christian holidays coincide with their Inca calendar.

The Quechua Indians are South American Indians who were conquered by the Inca and became part of their empire. Although centuries ago they may have resented the imperialism, they soon learned about its benefits, and today they proudly regard themselves as descendants of the Inca.

They live mainly in the Andean highlands of Peru, Bolivia, and Chile. They are farmers and, in the tradition of their forefathers, artisans that specialize in beautiful knit woolens, cotton fabrics, and hats.

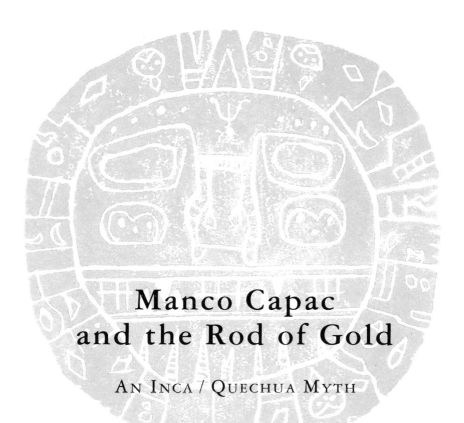

Manco Capac
and the Rod of Gold

An Inca / Quechua Myth

In the heart of every Inca lives an ancient story that comes to life in the rhythm of a song. It is to be passed along from generation to generation—and kept preserved through the years in their collective memory.

Long ago in ancient times, the Peruvian highlands were just craggy, bushy hills. The inhabitants of these lands were wild people who lived in small groups and hid in mountain caves. And like beasts, they ate grasses and roots and wild fruits. Sometimes they even ate human meat. They wore tree leaves and animal hides to cover themselves, or simply went naked.

One day, Father Sun took pity on these people who had no knowledge of farming or weaving. He sent his own son and daughter from the sky to help them learn the ways of the gods. They were to teach the people on earth how to work the land and live from the fruit of their labor; how to build dwellings and live in communities; and how to worship Father Sun and live by his law. With this command, he put his son and daughter in Lake Titicaca, and as a sign he gave them a thick golden rod about half the length of a man's arm. Then he spoke:

"Walk, my children, in any direction, and find a site for a city, and build it. Whenever you stop to eat or sleep, drive the rod into the ground. When

you find a place where the rod disappears in just one push, there you shall build the new kingdom."

Before they parted he added, "When all the people have become your subjects, you must rule them wisely and justly, with pity, with mercy, and with tenderness. Treat them with as much compassion as a father would treat his beloved children. It is in this way you must imitate me. For it is I who bring warmth and light to the world, watching over it lovingly as I circle it each day. I have sent you to the earth to save these people who live there as wild beasts. I therefore name you king and queen. You shall rule over all who will follow your guidance and your lawful government."

So it was that Father Sun left. Dressed as king and queen in regal garments and adorned with sumptuous earrings that would later become a sign of nobility among the Inca, the Sun's children began walking north. They traveled on foot for a long distance. Wherever they stopped to eat or sleep they would try to bury the rod in the ground, but without success. They continued their walk until they arrived in the Cuzco valley. In this rough land they stood, and the Sun's son tried to drive the rod into the ground once more. This time it went easily, and disappeared into the earth.

The Sun's son became the first Inca king and he said to his queen: "This must be the valley decreed by our Father Sun to be settled to fulfill his command. So it is wise, my queen and sister, that now we each part in search of the people who will follow the ways of our father and live according to his law. A temple dedicated to him shall be built in the heart of the city."

They both took different paths, spreading their father's word. The wild people, awed by the Inca king and his queen's rich appearance, were tempted by their promises of an enlightened community and plenty of food to eat. Hence, many men, women, and children followed the king. An equal number followed the queen. The king and queen became their rulers, and as they walked toward the valley of Cuzco, the number of followers increased twofold and threefold.

As the royal couple witnessed this, they stopped and said: "We shall divide the workload among all of us." Some were sent for food, others to build huts and houses. In this way, the imperial city was built. The king's followers settled in Hanan Cozco, the high Cuzco. The queen's followers settled in Hurin Cozco, the lower Cuzco.

While the city was being built, the king taught the men how to plow and farm the land, how to sow the seed into the ground, how to cultivate plants in rows, and how to know which ones to eat. He taught them what kind of tools to use, and how to build ditches to irrigate the fields. The Inca *rey*, the Inca king, taught the men all they needed to know, even how to make shoes.

The Inca *coya*, the Inca queen, busied herself in teaching all the women how to spin and knit cotton and wool, and also how to make clothes for themselves, their husbands, and their children. She showed them the best way to cook and clean and do every domestic chore. With grace and good will, the Inca king taught the men while the Inca queen taught the women. From them, the people learned all that was necessary to live a good life.

The Inca king was called Manco Capac, and his queen was called Mama Ocllo Huaco. They were children of the Sun and Moon, brother and sister, and the first royal couple of the great Inca empire from whom all other rulers would descend.

The tale of Manco Capac is still widespread among the Quechua and told in many variations. Many Indians strongly believe that one day, the Inca rey *will come back to Peru to restore the Inca rule.*

Kákuy

A QUECHUA FOLKTALE FROM BOLIVIA,
SIXTEENTH CENTURY

A long time ago, a young couple left their home and family and went to live in the middle of the jungle. There they built a hut. The man hunted and fished, and the woman picked all the wild fruit she could find. Soon they had two children, a boy and a girl.

One day, when the children were very young, the mother became ill with fever and died. A few years later the father was bitten by a poisonous snake and also passed away. The children were forced to live on their own.

The young boy learned how to hunt and fish as he had seen his father do, and he also collected wild fruits as he had seen his mother do. He provided his sister with everything she needed. He was a generous, kind, and peaceful boy. He was able to protect their hut from predators and was such a skillful hunter that he almost always returned from his hunting trips with a deer, an iguana, or at least a plump partridge. He was also quite good at finding beehives so that he could retrieve the delicious golden honey.

The sister, however, was quite different. She was cold, selfish, and very disagreeable. She didn't like to go out of the hut, and spent hours knitting inside. She didn't enjoy talking to her brother either, and only spoke to him to contradict or wound him with her words. She hated and despised him.

Nevertheless, the brother loved her, and he spoiled her with his attention.

He would bring her the sweetest honey, the juiciest wild fruits, the freshest fish, and the rarest partridge eggs. But the more he cared for her, the more she despised him.

I love her so, the brother thought to himself, *but nothing I do makes her happy. What could I do to make her love me as she should love a brother?* He anguished over these thoughts for weeks and months, but the sister only became more hostile and abusive. The brother was desperate.

Very late one evening, he returned from a hunting trip empty-handed. He had hunted for hours, but had very bad luck. His feet were bleeding and he was overcome with hunger and fatigue. The moment he entered the hut, his sister began cursing him, accusing him of being lazy and useless.

The brother was too exhausted to fight back, and instead he begged for a little water with honey for his thirst, and a *yuyu,* a mixture of soothing herbs, for his sore feet. She brought them, but instead of handing them to him, she threw the water on the dirt floor and the *yuyu* into the fire. Humiliated, the brother silently walked to a corner of the hut and fell asleep.

The next morning he awoke still hungry and in pain. He slowly cooked some food for himself but before it was done, his sister maliciously grabbed the pot and threw the food far into the woods. The boy could not believe his eyes. It was then he decided he would not take his sister's abuse any longer.

He thought about abandoning her—or even killing her. But he realized he still loved her. After all, she was his sister.

Then he thought of a plan that would surely teach her a lesson.

First he went into the jungle in search of a *murumuru* hive. The *murumuru* is a tiny bee that is as feared for its painful sting as it is sought after for its exquisite honey. And it was a delicacy that his sister delighted in. He found the perfect hive that was so high up in the trees he had to go back to the hut to get his sister to help him. Reluctantly, she agreed to help, and they set out on their journey together. They walked far into the depths of the jungle, leaving the tiny hut very far behind. When they arrived at the tall tree, the brother examined the trunk and the branches carefully.

"No, we can't go up," he said finally. "The tree trunk is far too wide and the beehive is much too high. It is plainly impossible. We should forget this plan and return home at once."

His sister was so stubborn that the thought of not being able to get the honey made her desire it all the more.

"I'll go by myself," she said. "I could climb even higher than the beehive, if I wanted to."

"If you insist," her brother said. "I'll go with you. We will help each other."

So they started to climb, the girl first, the boy following behind. The branches were so far apart that it was impossible for one to climb without the other's help. Once they were close to the beehive, the brother told his sister to cover her face to protect herself from the fierce stings of the *murumuru*. These bees lived in colonies of thousands and would attack mercilessly. They would go right for the face, stinging it painfully until it became deformed.

Fearing the bee's attack, the sister took off her shawl and carefully wrapped it around her head, face, and neck. Then she waited for further instructions from her brother. But after a strange silence, she suddenly realized her brother was gone. She was all alone at the top of the tree! Filled with terror, she removed the shawl as her eyes darted quickly around the jungle. For an instant, she thought she saw her brother's silhouette blending in with the darkness. It was at that moment that the bees began their assault. Instantly she tried to climb down, but to her surprise, the trunk was bare! All of the tree branches had been cut off. There was no way down. Desperately she said a prayer. She thought she was saying:

> *Don't abandon me, my brother,*
> *stay next to me.*
> *Don't leave me without your protection.*

But her throat could only emit two short words:

> *Kákuy, turay . . .*
> *Kákuy, turay . . .*
> *Kákuy, turay . . .*

which, in Quechua, means, "Stay, my brother."

As the dusk fell softly over the jungle, the selfish girl, with disfigured face, hands, and feet, wished fervently that her prayers might reach her brother's ears. Later, feeling hopeless and exhausted, she was overcome with the desire to turn into a bird. In the black of the night, she implored the gods to allow her to fly in search of her brother. The gods heard her. Soon she felt herself diminish in size, and her feet curl into claws. She felt her arms fold into wings and her skin grow dense and dark as feathers sprouted from it. But alas! As she spread her wings to fly, she discovered she could only fly a short distance, from tree to tree, from branch to branch. And as she flew, she pleadingly sang:

> *Kákuy, turay . . .*
> *Kákuy, turay . . .*
> *Kákuy, turay . . .*

To this day, when the deep silence of the night in the Chaco is broken by a plaintive bird song, you will know that this is the song of the kákuy. Peasants say that nobody has ever seen the bird that hides in the day and hunts for food in the dark of the night. But all have heard it proclaim its presence with its tearful song—forever filling the Bolivian night with sadness.

The Courier

A QUECHUA LEGEND FROM BOLIVIA, SIXTEENTH CENTURY

When José Wallulu, an Indian also known as Josucho, turned eighteen, he was chosen by the authorities to be a *chasqui*, a courier. As courier, he would run with messages between his town and the capital.

Early one morning the mayor knocked on his door and gave him two urgent letters that were to be delivered immediately. Quickly Josucho put on his cloth cap, tied a blanket to his poncho, and prepared some lunch meat, cold potatoes, toasted corn, and coca leaves. Then, grabbing his walking stick, he started on his way.

For hours he climbed the slopes, following the winding path that led to the peak of the mountains that surrounded the village. He stopped to catch his breath and lay down on the edge of the cliff. From this height, he could see the small houses in the distance, the thin threads of smoke coming from within them, and the villagers, who looked like tiny specks of color, going about their business.

Seeing the Apachita, the stone mound that was dedicated to the spirit of the mountain, he spat some of his coca on the ground, stood up, and continued up the hill to make an offering at the altar. Upon reaching it, he picked up a stone from the road and began to say a prayer that the local priest had taught him.

Just as he was about to offer the stone, however, he noticed an *allqö*, a strange hairy dog, sitting on his hind legs next to the altar. As the dog stared quietly at the stone mound, Josucho wanted to run in fear, as he had been warned by his grandmother that this was a very bad omen. Instead, he took out his slingshot and hit the dog on the hip with the stone he had meant as his offering. The dog let out a pitiful scream and limped all the way into the solitude of the *pampas*, the South American plains.

It was getting late in the afternoon as Josucho hurried along through the Andean highlands. He scanned the landscape below and took in all the lonely immensity of his green and magnificent *pampas*. Above him the sky was threatening rain and he thought it would be better to get to the lodge before nightfall. Suddenly, a beautiful young girl appeared before him. She was dressed in a white blouse and a flowing black skirt, and her hat was tipped coquettishly to one side. In her hands she wound black yarn into a ball.

Josucho approached her, hoping that perhaps she would accompany him on the remainder of his journey.

"Are you going to Ayllukullama?" he asked the girl.

"Yes," she replied. "And yourself, Josucho?"

Josucho was bewildered. "How do you know my name?" he stammered, for he had never seen the girl before.

"I'm Naticha," the girl answered. "We used to play hide-and-seek when we were children."

Josucho was still startled by the strange girl, and even a bit frightened of her. But she was so pretty that he soon forgot his uneasiness and could think of nothing but how much he wished to kiss her.

The night crept in softly, and the warm air turned to cold when Josucho decided it was time to stop for the day. He feared the dangers of travel at night. With no light to guide them, there was the possibility of getting lost or inadvertently stepping into a marsh. Having been distracted by the girl's talk, he lost track of time and was farther from the lodge than he had intended to be. So he invited Naticha to stop and rest with him. He took out his cold food and shared it with the bewitching girl.

As they ate their meal, he thought of how pleasant and special this night would be, sleeping on the thick grass, in the midst of the mountain. The velvet black sky was bursting with stars that glittered above them.

They lay on his poncho on the grass, and when the night grew colder, they covered themselves with his blanket. As they huddled close to one another he drew her near and began to kiss her. But when Josucho's hand accidentally brushed against her hip she pulled herself away from him and screamed, *"Ayy ay ayy!* Don't touch me there! It hurts where you hit me with the rock!"

Josucho looked at her blankly.

"Earlier today in the Apachita, I sat next to you at the stone altar when you hit me mercilessly with your slingshot."

An icy chill shot through Josucho as he remembered the earlier incident with the strange dog. Whirling through his mind were the dog's painful screams, the sudden appearance of Naticha later on, and the echos of his grandmother's many eerie stories about the strange, hairy *allqös*.

Panic and fear raced through him as the terrifying truth emerged.

"Auuuuuuuu!" the suddenly sinister Naticha howled. And in a moment the young girl twisted and writhed and then transformed into a snarling mad dog.

The dog crept toward Josucho, its mouth foaming, its eyes glistening with a ferocious glint that was intently fixed on his face.

Josucho got up instantly and as the stars watched from above, they were the only witnesses of his swift escape into the shadows of the Andean highlands.

The villagers of Ayllukullama were stunned when the *chasqui* told them what had happened. After a long, relentless hunt, they caught the hairy dog some days later. They lit a large bonfire on the main street, and without pity threw the dog in and burned it alive. And as they watched the animal go up in flames, they realized it was a girl possessed—and transformed into an *allqö*.

It was a great honor to be selected as a chasqui *during the Inca Empire. These special couriers had the important task of delivering the messages from the Inca to the governors. The young Indian boys who were chosen for this job not only had to be the fastest runners, but they also needed to possess a talent for memorizing a spoken message and reading the one recorded in a code of colored yarns and different knots, called* quipu. *Without conventional writing, the success of the empire depended on the communication provided by these relays of post runners who traveled the vast road system that connected all corners of the realm.*

Now, hundreds of years have passed,
and the chasquis *run no more.*
Gone is the gold, once easily had,
though its sparkle still remains—
in the poetry of words
from the countless voices heard.
The ancient stories,
kept alive in our collective memories,
are the Golden Tales
inherited from the lands of Latin America.

Notes and Sources

The memories of the legends and folktales I heard and read as a child still live in my heart today. The powerful love of the beautiful Taino princess and her Spanish warrior mesmerized me as I struggled to comprehend emotions I had not yet felt. The strength and persistence of the Puerto Rican people defending the capital city from the English in 1797 instilled within me a pride I still hold. And my desire to learn more about the ever-present but elusive Taino made me realize that there was, perhaps, more to know than what I had been taught. So it was my wish to rediscover the literature that had shaped my early perceptions and the desire to pass these stories along to my children that inspired me to write *Golden Tales*.

To begin my research, I first went back to the original versions of the stories I so fondly remembered. Then I looked for others as beautiful and compelling to add to this collection. In my quest for specific tales, I traveled to Mexico and Puerto Rico, and conducted research at the Library of Congress in Washington, D.C., as well as at the Instituto Nacional de Antropología e Historia in Mexico City. Since many of the original versions of the tales that were written in old Spanish were not meant for children, I also had the challenge of retelling them in a way that would appeal to today's young readers.

In the course of my investigations, I read and studied material that would later help me in creating the art. Because I needed to convey the mystery and the magic that many of the tales possess, I decided to paint in oils. And in my effort to get even closer to the art forms used by the specific indigenous cultures, I used linocuts to reproduce some of the early design motifs that had originally been carved into bone, stone, and wood — or woven into cloth. I have included the following notes to extend the reader's understanding of the stories and pictures in this collection, and to cite their sources.

The Cover
THE ART
• The map on the cover represents the Americas as the Spaniards believed them to be around the year 1500. I based this illustration on a *mappamundi*, a map of the world, by Juan de la Cosa.
• The oil painting on the front cover: see note for "How the Sea Was Born," page 5.

• The oil painting on the back cover: see art note for "From the Land of the Muisca."
• The ornate "G" in the title and the border are based on elements from Spanish illuminated manuscripts from the 1400s.
SOURCES
LEVENSON, JAY A., ed. *Circa 1492, Art in the Age of Exploration*. Washington, D.C.: National Gallery of Art, New Haven & London: Yale University Press, 1991.

Introduction
THE ART
• Although I rendered the map on page iv in a fifteenth-century style, the contours of the continents, as well as the countries' boundaries, are modern.

FROM THE LANDS OF THE TAINO
THE ART
• The oil painting on page vi depicts some of the food crops that the Taino introduced to the Europeans, as well as some of the Taino words that are now part of the Spanish language.
• The linocut border on page 1 is a motif that represents rain and water. The symbol appears in a Taino "stone collar," a stone belt used by players in a Taino ball game.
SOURCES
FERNÁNDEZ MÉNDEZ, EUGENIO. *Art and Mythology of the Taino Indians of the Greater West Indies*. San Juan, Puerto Rico: Ediciones El Cemí, 1993.
HERNÁNDEZ AQUINO, LUIS. *Diccionario de voces indígenas de Puerto Rico*. Bilbao, España: Editorial Vasco Americana, 1969.
ROUSE, IRVING. *The Tainos, Rise and Decline of the People Who Greeted Columbus*. New Haven and London: Yale University Press, 1992.

How the Sea Was Born
THE TALE
I based my retelling on Pané's chronicles of the Taino myths. Ramón Pané was a friar who came to the Americas with Columbus. At Columbus's request, Pané collected and recorded Taino myths and traditions during his stay in Hispaniola.
SOURCES
PANÉ, RAMÓN. *Relación acerca de las antigüedades de los indios*. México: Siglo XXI, 1978. Versión por José Juan Arrom.

THE ART
• The oil painting on page 2 shows a Taino funerary urn carved in wood and found in Cuba. Chroniclers say the Taino hung urns, baskets, or gourds containing the bones of their ancestors from a post inside their *bohíos*, their huts. It is said that they

believed in the afterlife and in communication with the dead.

• The linocut on page 3 is a motif found carved into rocks at La Piedra Escrita near Jayuya, Puerto Rico.

• In the oil painting on page 4, the feminine figure represents Itiba Cahubaba, Mother Earth. It was taken from a Taino sculpted clay cup from Santo Domingo. The open bowl was modeled after one found in Vieques, Puerto Rico.

• The figure in the oil painting on page 5 (also shown on the cover) depicts the top of another sculpted clay cup from Santo Domingo. It represents Deminán Caracaracol. The fish are tropical species found in the Caribbean coral reefs.

SOURCES

ARROM, JOSÉ JUAN. *Mitología y artes prehispánicas de las Antillas.* México: Siglo XXI, 1975.

FERNÁNDEZ MÉNDEZ, EUGENIO. *Art and Mythology of the Taino Indians of the Greater West Indies.* San Juan, Puerto Rico: Ediciones El Cemí, 1993.

Guanina
THE TALE

This tragic love story, masterfully told by nineteenth-century author Cayetano Coll y Toste, was my most compelling inspiration for creating this book. In my version I retell the story in language more accessible to modern-day children. I also attempt to shed light on the feelings of the character Guanina.

SOURCES

COLL Y TOSTE, CAYETANO. *Leyendas y tradiciones puertorriqueñas.* Puerto Rico: Editorial Cultural, 1975.

THE ART

• Both Taino men and women painted their bodies with black, red, and white natural dyes. They adorned themselves with necklaces and bracelets made out of shells, small pebbles, bones, and feathers. They wore strips of cotton cloth tied to their wrists and ankles. Married Taino women wore small cotton aprons called *naguas.* Since Guanina was Don Cristóbal's loved one, I took the liberty of covering her upper body on page 6. After all, if he'd taught her to braid her hair in the Castilian style, I imagined he would not have been indifferent to her partial nakedness.

• The linocut on page 7 is a twin motif that was carved on a wooden *dúho,* a chief's stool.

• During the colonization of Puerto Rico that took place between 1508 and 1511, the first soldiers were mounted knights dressed in suits of armor. The Museum in San Felipe del Morro, San Juan, Puerto Rico, houses a suit of armor like the one in the painting on page 11.

SOURCES

ALEGRÍA, RICARDO. *Historia de nuestros indios.* San Juan, Puerto Rico: Colección de Estudios Puertorriqueños, 1969.

FERNÁNDEZ MÉNDEZ, EUGENIO. *Art and Mythology*

of the Taino Indians of the Greater West Indies. San Juan, Puerto Rico: Ediciones El Cemí, 1993.

The Eleven Thousand Virgins
THE TALE

Old San Juan, Puerto Rico is filled with historic places, many of which are shrouded in the magic of legend. Growing up on the island, I heard the legend of "The Eleven Thousand Virgins," and I passed it along to my own children as we walked the cobblestone streets in front of the San Juan Cathedral. The English attack is well documented in history books, and it forms part of the curriculum for schoolchildren in Puerto Rico.

SOURCES

BLANCO, ENRIQUE T. *Los tres ataques británicos a la ciudad de San Juan Bautista de Puerto Rico.* San Juan, Puerto Rico: Editorial Coquí, 1968.

COLL Y TOSTE, CAYETANO. *Leyendas y tradiciones puertorriqueñas.* Puerto Rico: Editorial Cultural, 1975.

THE ART

• The map on page 14 of the northern part of the island of Puerto Rico is based on 1783 plans for the San Juan fortifications. The English general represents Sir Ralph Abercromby.

• The linocut on page 15 is a Taino motif carved on a wooden *dúho,* or chief's stool, probably alluding to Venus.

• The oil painting on page 17 depicts the Calle de las Monjas in Old San Juan, Puerto Rico, a street leading to the San Juan Cathedral.

• La Rogativa, on page 19, is a bronze sculpture that stands near the gate of San Juan. It commemorates the time the city was saved from the English attack in 1797.

SOURCES

FERNÁNDEZ MÉNDEZ, EUGENIO. *Art and Mythology of the Taino Indians of the Greater West Indies.* San Juan, Puerto Rico: Ediciones El Cemí, 1993.

TAYLOR, RENÉ. *José Campeche and His Time.* Ponce, Puerto Rico: Museo de Arte de Ponce, 1988.

The Laughing Skull
THE TALE

It was a Dominican friend who directed me to the collection of Dominican traditions, historic tales, and anecdotes by Troncoso de la Concha. The author was born in 1878 and was president of the Dominican Republic from 1940 to 1942. I loved his version of the tale for its unexpected and humorous ending.

SOURCES

TRONCOSO DE LA CONCHA, MANUEL. *Narraciones dominicanas.* Santo Domingo: Editora de Santo Domingo, 1977.

THE ART

• On page 20 I have shown colonial buildings in Santo Domingo, Dominican Republic.

• The linocut on page 21 shows a carved face from

a Taino bone vessel from the Dominican Republic.

SOURCES

ROUSE, IRVING. *The Tainos, Rise and Decline of the People Who Greeted Columbus.* New Haven & London: Yale University Press, 1992.

UGARTE, MARÍA. *Monumentos coloniales.* Santo Domingo: Publicaciones del Museo de las Casas Reales, 1977.

Sención, the Indian Girl

THE TALE

The young girl in this tale is a mixture of three races: Indian, black, and white. After several years of forced labor by the Spaniards, the indigenous population began to diminish, and in the year 1518, Africans were brought to the islands to work as slaves. In time, all three races mixed to become the Caribbean people of today.

SOURCES

BUENO, SALVADOR, ed. *Leyendas cubanas.* La Habana, Cuba: Editorial Arte y Literatura, 1975.

THE ART

• The linocut on page 25 shows a twin motif as it appears in a Taino "stone collar," a stone belt used by players in a Taino ball game.

SOURCES

FERNÁNDEZ MÉNDEZ, EUGENIO. *Art and Mythology of the Taino Indians of the Greater West Indies.* San Juan, Puerto Rico: Ediciones El Cemí, 1993.

FROM THE LAND OF THE ZAPOTEC

THE ART

• The oil painting on page 28 shows a contemporary Zapotec Indian market that takes place in the middle of a colonial town in the state of Oaxaca, Mexico. Modern-day Zapotec girls help their families by weaving ribbons and belts on their back strap looms. The border around the painting is based on a hand-woven hair ribbon made by one of the young girls who posed for this picture.

• The linocut border on page 29 shows the rain motif that is part of the beautiful geometric stonework mosaics adorning the walls of Mitla, an ancient Zapotec city in the state of Oaxaca.

SOURCES

SCHEFFLER, LILIAN. *Los indígenas mexicanos.* México: Panorama Editorial, 1992.

Personal travel and interviews.

When the Sun and the Moon Were Children

THE TALE

I first encountered this tale in Bierhorst's *The Mythology of Mexico and Central America.* I decided to go to the source myself, and on a trip to Mexico had the opportunity not only to read the original version at the Instituto Nacional de Antropología e Historia, but to visit Oaxaca, the land of the

Zapotec and Chatino.

SOURCES

BARTOLOMÉ, MIGUEL ALBERTO. *Narrativa y etnicidad entre los chatinos de Oaxaca.* México: INAH, 1979.

THE ART

• On page 30, the woman and children are Chatino Indians, dressed in the traditional garments that are still worn today.

• The linocut on page 31 shows a solar disk motif from a gold pendant found in the tombs of Monte Albán, Oaxaca, the ancient capital of the Zapotec state.

• The rabbit in the full moon on page 35 is a common motif used throughout Mexico.

SOURCES

COE, MICHAEL D. *Mexico, from the Olmecs to the Aztecs.* London: Thames and Hudson, 1962.

Photos taken by the author.

How the Rainbow Was Born

THE TALE

In Oaxaca, I met a man who was the proud son of a Zapotec Indian woman and a Spanish man. He told me his version of "How the Rainbow Was Born" as he explained the symbolism of the stonework in Mitla. Later, I found a collection by Otilia Meza that provided me with a more complete version, which I have retold here.

SOURCES

MEZA, OTILIA. *Leyendas prehispánicas mexicanas.* Mexico: Panorama Editorial, 1992.

THE ART

• On page 36, the god of lightning, the master of rain, is based on a funerary vessel from Monte Albán that represents the rain god. The geometric motifs behind the god, from top to bottom, represent clouds, hail, rain, and wind. They were taken from the stonework at Mitla.

• The linocut on page 37 is a motif that was carved in bone and found in a tomb in Monte Albán.

• Page 39 shows a view from the north façade of the Building of Columns in Mitla, Oaxaca. Mitla is known to the Zapotec as the place of rest. It was still in use when the Spaniards arrived. Mitla is a city of unparalleled beauty where native Zapotec ceremonies are still carried out within its precincts — side by side with Christian rites.

SOURCES

COE, MICHAEL D. *Mexico, from the Olmecs to the Aztecs.* London: Thames and Hudson, 1962.

Photos taken by the author.

The Miracle of Our Lady of Guadalupe

THE TALE

On my visit to Mexico City, I went to the Villa de Guadalupe. There, my Mexican guide told me the legend of the Virgin. Although I was already familiar with the miracle, listening to his words while looking at the church where Juan Diego's cloak still hangs gave the story a new dimension.

THE ART

• I based the oil painting on page 40 on photographs I took at the Villa de Guadalupe. And while painting Juan Diego's face, I kept pictures of Diego Rivera's murals pinned to my easel for inspiration.

• The linocut on page 41 is an embroidery motif from a Zapotec *huipil,* the traditional women's garment.

• The church on page 43 is the Old Basilica of Guadalupe, which was finished in 1709. It was here that the image of the Virgin was kept until the recent construction of a very large and innovative new basilica.

SOURCES
Photos taken by the author at Museo Regional de Oaxaca and Villa de Guadalupe.

FROM THE LAND OF THE MUISCA

THE ART

• The painting on page 44 (also shown on the back cover) depicts gold *tunjos* laying over a leaf. The Muisca Indians were skilled goldsmiths who paid homage to the sun and the water. The *tunjos* were not items of jewelry, but rather offerings to the gods, created to be hidden away in sacred places. They usually represented people, animals, and tools of the everyday world in accurate detail. The offerings were made through the chiefs or priests. The border surrounding the painting shows gold figurines representing serpents.

• The linocut border on page 45 is a design motif from a cylindrical Muisca stamp, believed to be used in the decoration of cloth and of the body.

SOURCES
PÉREZ DE BARRADAS, JOSÉ. *Los muiscas antes de la conquista.* Madrid: Consejo Superior de Investigaciones Científicas. Instituto Bernardino de Sahagún, 1950.

El Dorado

THE TALE

This is probably the best-known legend from Latin America. It attracted many Europeans who came to the new world in search of gold and El Dorado, the mythical land filled with riches.

Pedro Simón (1574–1630) was a Spanish friar who studied the Muisca and chronicled the myth of the goddess Bachué. He describes how the Muisca people were born from the union of this goddess and a boy she retrieved from a lagoon. He goes on to tell how, after populating the lands, the boy and the goddess turned into serpents and returned to the lake. Simón also chronicled the myth

of the Muisca chief and his wife, the legend of El Dorado, and the historic events describing the accomplishments of the Spaniard Sebastián de Benalcázar.

Later, Pérez de Barradas analyzed Simón's chronicles and theorized that the myth of the chief's wife was the event that gave origin to the ritual described in the legend of "El Dorado." But the wrenching drama of the Muisca chief's wife usually does not appear in the legend. I added it to my version, in light of Barradas's and Cano's beliefs, and set this retelling in the historic frame of Benalcázar's accomplishments.

SOURCES
ARANGO CANO, JESÚS. *Mitos, leyendas y dioses chibchas.* Bogotá, Colombia: Plaza & Janés, 1985.
PÉREZ DE BARRADAS, JOSÉ. *Los muiscas antes de la conquista.* Madrid: Consejo Superior de Investigaciones Científicas, Instituto Bernardino de Sahagún, 1950.
SIMÓN, FRAY PEDRO, b. 1574. *Noticias historiales sobre el Reino de Nueva Granada.* Bogotá, Colombia: Ministerio de Educación Nacional Ediciones de la Revista Bolívar, 1953.

THE ART

• The painting on page 46 shows the Guatavita Lagoon.

• The linocut on page 47 is based on a Muisca ceramic figure holding offerings that is housed in El Museo del Oro, Bogotá, Colombia.

• Much information on the traditions, garments, headdresses, and corporal adornments of the Muisca has been collected by chroniclers. Men and women pierced their ears. They wore white and bright-colored cotton garments. On special occasions they decorated their bodies with paint and wore headdresses made of animal hides or colorful cotton flowers. Only the warriors cropped their hair and pierced the outer edges of their ears as well as their lips, where they placed small tubes of gold for each enemy killed. The raft shown in the painting on pages 50–51 is based on a gold replica of the original one, also currently housed in El Museo del Oro, Bogotá.

• The sword pictured on page 51 is from Spain.

SOURCES
LEVENSON, JAY A., ed. *Circa 1492, Art in the Age of Exploration.* Washington, D.C.: National Gallery of Art, New Haven & London: Yale University Press, 1991.
PÉREZ DE BARRADAS, JOSÉ. *Los muiscas antes de la conquista.* Madrid: Consejo Superior de Investigaciones Científicas, Instituto Bernardino de Sahagún, 1950.

FROM THE LANDS OF THE QUECHUA, CHILDREN OF THE INCA

THE ART

• The painting on page 52 shows modern-day Quechua Indians in the city of Cuzco. Precisely fitted Inca stone masonry has resisted conquests and earthquakes alike for more than 500 years. Atop

such stones, the Spaniards built their own structures that in some cases have been tumbled several times by quakes. The Indian in the foreground is playing the *zampoña,* the pan pipe, and the *bombo* drum. He wears *chajchas,* a bracelet made of goat's toenails, which is also a percussion instrument. In the border surrounding the painting, there are motifs from an Inca tunic. Usually rulers or members of the royal family wore tunics with these motifs.
• The linocut on page 53 shows the black-and-white checker motif from tunics worn by Inca soldiers.

SOURCES
LEVENSON, JAY A., ed. *Circa 1492, Art in the Age of Exploration.* Washington, D.C.: National Gallery of Art, New Haven & London: Yale University Press, 1991.

Manco Capac and the Rod of Gold

THE TALE

In the best-known creation myth of the Inca, the god Wirakocha emerged from Lake Titicaca and proceeded to the site of Cuzco, where he spoke to a man named Manco Capac, charging him to rule the empire. However, the story of the founding of the empire is told differently by Garcilaso de la Vega, who was the son of an Inca princess and a Spanish soldier. He wrote the tale of the founding of Cuzco by drawing from the traditional lore that he had heard as a child. This version appeared in his *Royal Commentaries of the Incas,* published in 1609. Having studied his work as a young girl in Puerto Rico, I chose to use his version in this book.

SOURCES
BIERHORST, JOHN, ed. *The Mythology of South America.* New York: Morrow, 1988.
GARCILASO DE LA VEGA, el Inca (1539–1616). *Leyendas y hechos fabulosos del antiguo Perú.* Lima: Ediciones Nuevo Mundo, 1962.

THE ART

• In the oil painting on page 54, Manco Capac and his sister-wife, Mama Ocllo Huaco, walk toward the valley of Cuzco. In the background is the Island of the Sun in Lake Titicaca. They are wearing Inca tunics, which are based on original ones that are still intact. They also have their ears pierced, a sign of nobility among the Inca.
• The linocut on page 55 depicts the Inca zodiac.
• The illustration on page 57 is an aerial view of Machu Picchu, a citadel unknown to the Spanish and discovered intact in 1911. This spectacular remnant of the Inca empire, encrusted with shrines, fountains, lodgings, and steep stairways, rises some 2,000 feet above the Urubamba River in Peru.

SOURCES
National Geographic Magazine (February 1971, December 1973). Washington, D.C.: National Geographic Society.
NEWMAN, SHIRLEE P. *The Incas.* New York: Franklin Watts, 1992.

Kákuy

THE TALE

The mystery of metamorphosis is very present in tales from the South American jungle. The story of the *kákuy* has been retold by both Argentinian and Bolivian writers. It may remind us of the magical realism frequently found in contemporary Latin American literature.

SOURCES
LARA, JESÚS. *Leyendas quechuas. Antología.* La Paz, Bolivia: Ediciones Librería Juventud, 1960.

THE ART

• The oil painting on page 58 shows the South American jungle.
• The linocut on page 59 is based on a nobleman's earring, crafted in gold and turquoise, found in a Moche tomb in Peru.
• The painting on page 62 depicts the transformation of the selfish girl into my interpretation of the mysterious nocturnal bird of the Chaco, *nyctibius jamaicensis,* commonly called *kákuy.*
• The oil painting on page 63 depicts night in the Bolivian Chaco, which is a semi-arid area next to the northern rain forest in the Oriente region of Bolivia.

SOURCES
National Geographic Magazine (October 1988). Washington, D.C.: National Geographic Society.

The Courier

THE TALE

This tale takes place during colonial times when *chasquis,* the Inca couriers or post runners, no longer had the status they had in the time of the great empire. Since it brings the reader closer in time to modern-day Quechua, I felt this tale was a fitting one to end the journey that started in the lands of the Taino.

SOURCES
LARA, JESÚS. *Mitos, leyendas y cuentos de los quechuas.* La Paz, Bolivia: Editorial Los Amigos del Libro, 1973.

THE ART

• The oil painting on page 64 shows a view of the Andean Plateau. Present-day highland Indians still wear hand-woven caps similar to those used during colonial times to protect themselves from the cold air of the highlands.
• The linocut on page 65 shows a motif from an early colonial Peruvian tunic.
• The royal Inca highways pictured on page 68 are still traveled by modern-day Indians. Along such roads, relays of *chasquis* once sped messages to keep the emperor in touch with his realm.

SOURCES
National Geographic Magazine (December 1978). Washington, D.C.: National Geographic Society.

Pronunciation Guide***

Agüeybana (Taino/Spanish) • ah-gway-BAH-nah, 7

Alfau, Abad (Spanish) • ah-BAHD AHL-fow, 22

Allqö (Quechua/Spanish) • AHL-ko, 66

Apachita (Quechua/Spanish) • ah-pah-CHEE-tah, 65

Arahuaco (Taino/Spanish) • ah-rah-WAH-ko, 1

Areito (Taino/Spanish) • ah-ray-EE-toe, 8

Ascensión (Spanish) • ah-sehn-see-OWN, 25

Atahualpa (Quechua/Spanish) • ah-tah-WAHL-pah, 53

Ayllukullama (Quechua) • i-u-ku-LYAH-mah, 66

Aztecs (Náhuatl/English) • AHZ-teks, 29

Bachué (Chibcha/Spanish) • bah-choo-AY, 47

Barrios (Spanish) • BAH-rryos, 45

Boca de Cangrejos (Spanish) • BO-cah DAY kahn-GRAY-hos, 15

Bohío (Taino/Spanish) • bo-EE-o, 3

Boriquén (Taino/Spanish) • bo-ree-KEHN, 7

Cacique (Taino/Spanish) • kah-SEE-kay, 1

Ceiba (Taino/Spanish) • SAYE-bah, 12

Cemí (Taino/Spanish) • seh-MEE, 10

Chaco (Quechua/Spanish) • CHAH-ko, 63

Chasqui (Quechua/Spanish) • CHAHS-kee, 65

Chatino (Spanish) • chah-TEE-no, 29

Chibcha (Chibcha/Spanish) • CHEEB-chah, 45

Chicha (Quechua) • CHEE-chah, 49

Cholos (Spanish) • CHO-los, 53

Condado (Spanish) • kon-DAH-do, 16

Conquistador (Spanish) • kohn-kees-tah-DOR, 7

Conuco (Taino/Spanish) • ko-NEW-ko, 4

Cosijogui (Zapotec) • ko-see-HO-gee, 37

Coya (Quechua/Spanish) • KOY-ah, 57

Cuzco (Quechua/Spanish) • KOOZ-koh, 53

de Benalcázar, Sebastián (Spanish) • se-bahs-tee-YAHN DAY bay-nahl-KAH-thahr, 47

de Castro, Don Ramón (Spanish) • DOAN rah-MOAN DAY KAH-strow, 15

de Sotomayor, Don Cristóbal (Spanish) • DOAN cree-STO-bahl DAY so-toe-my-YOUR, 7

Deminán Caracaracol (Taino/Spanish) • deh-mee-NAHN kah-RAH-kah-RAH-kohl, 4

Diego, Juan (Spanish) • HWAHN dee-AY-go, 41

El Dorado (Spanish) • EHL do-RAH-do, 47

Gabicha (Zapotec) • gah-BEE-chah, 38

González, Juan (Spanish) • HWAHN gohn-THAH-lehth, 8

Guadalupe (Spanish) • gwah-dah-LOO-pay, 41

Guanín (Taino/Spanish) • gwah-NEEN, 10

Guanina (Taino/Spanish) • gwah-NEE-nah, 7

Guatavita (Chibcha/Spanish) • GWAH-tah-VEE-tah, 47

Guaybana (Taino/Spanish) • gway-BAH-nah, 9

Hanan Cozco (Quechua) • HAH-nahn KUS-ko, 57

Hurin Cozco (Quechua) • HU-reen KUS-ko, 57

Inca (Quechua/Spanish) • EEN-kah, v, 53

Itiba Cahubaba (Taino/Spanish) • ee-TEE-bah ka-oo-BAH-bah, 4

Jeques (Chibcha/Spanish) • HEH-kays, 48

Josucho (Spanish) • ho-ZOO-cho, 65

Juárez, Benito (Spanish) • beh-NEE-toe HWAH-res, 29

Kákuy (Quechua/Spanish) • KAH-kooey, 61

Kákuy, turay (Quechua) • KAH-kooey too-RI, 61

Luna (Spanish) • LOO-nah, 31

Machu Picchu (Quechua/Spanish) • MAH-choo PEE-choo, 53

Mama Ocllo Huaco (Quechua/Spanish) • MAH-mah OHK-lyo WAH-co, 57

Mamaíta (Spanish) • mah-mah-EE-tah, 26

Manco Capac (Quechua) • MAHN-koe KAH-pahk, 57

Maya (Maya/Spanish) • MAH-yah, 29

Miramar (Spanish) • mee-rah-MAHR, 16

Mitla (Náhuatl/Spanish) • MEET-lah, 29

Mixtecs (Náhuatl) • MEES-teks, 29

Monte Albán (Spanish) • MON-tay ahl-BAHN, 29

Muisca (Spanish) • MWEE-skah, v, 45

Murumuru (Quechua) • MOO-roo-MOO-roo, 60

Naborias (Taino/Spanish) • nah-BO-reeahz, 9

Naticha (Spanish) • nah-TEE-chah, 66

Oaxaca (Spanish) • wah-HAH-kah, 29

Pampas (Quechua/Spanish) • PAHM-pahs, 66

Pitao (Zapotec) • pee-TAU, 38

Ponce de León, Juan (Spanish) • HWAHN PON-thay DAY ley-ON, 13

Quechua (Quechua/Spanish) • KEH-chwah, 53

Quipu (Quechua/Spanish) • KEE-pu, 68

Rey (Spanish) • RAY, 57

Rogativa (Spanish) • ro-gah-TEE-vah, 16

Sagua la Grande (Spanish) • SAH-gwah LA GRAHN-day, 25

San Antonio (Spanish) • SAHN ahn-TO-neeoh, 15

San Gerónimo (Spanish) • SAHN hay-RO-nee-mo, 16

San Juan (Spanish) • SAHN HWAHN, 15

Santo Domingo (Spanish) • SAHN-to do-MING-o, 21

Sención (Spanish) • sehn-see-OWN, 25

Skualyku (Chatino) • SKWA-li-ku, 33

Sol (Spanish) • SOHL, 31

Suliuu (Chatino) • su-lee-OO, 34

Taino (Taino/Spanish) • tah-EE-no, v, 1

Tamales (Náhuatl/Spanish) • tah-MAH-lehs, 35

Te Deum (Latin) • TAY DAY-yum, 18

Tepeyac (Náhuatl/Spanish) • teh-pay-AHK, 41

Titicaca (Quechua/Spanish) • tee-tee-KAH-kah, 55

Tonantzin (Náhuatl/Spanish) • to-nahnt-THEEN, 41

Tortillas (Spanish) • tohr-TEE-lyahs, 35

Trespalacios (Spanish) • TRES-pah-LAH-thyos, 15

Villa Caparra (Spanish) • VEE-lyah ka-PAH-rrah, 8

Villa de Guadalupe (Spanish) • VEE-lyah DAY gwah-dah-LOO-pay, 43

Viva (Spanish) • VEE-vah, 11

Wallullu, José (Spanish) • ho-THAY wah-LYOO-lyoo, 65

Yaya (Taino/Spanish) • YAH-yah, 3

Yayael (Taino/Spanish) • yah-yah-ALE, 3

Yucca (Taino/English) • YOO-kah, 4

Yuyu (Quechua/Spanish) • YOO-yoo, 60

Zapotec (Zapotec/English) • ZAH-po-tek, v, 29

Zumárraga (Spanish) • thu-MAH-rrah-gah, 41

*Page numbers indicate where words appear in context in the text, often with definitions.

**Spanish pronunciations are Castilian to reflect the Spanish that would have been spoken during the time of Columbus.